Your favourite pin-ups

GW00507433

☆ Margaret Lockwood ☆

(1916 -1990)

REMEMBER HOW BEAUTY SPOTS BECAME
BIG BUSINESS IN THE 1940S AS
YOUNG WOMEN IN BRITAIN COPIED
THEIR FAVOURITE FILM STAR
MARGARET LOCKWOOD?
SHE MADE HER FILM DEBUT IN 'LORNA
DOONE' IN 1934. 'THE LADY VANISHES'
FOR ALFRED HITCHCOCK FOLLOWED AND,
BACK IN BRITAIN, 'THE WICKED LADY'
CONFIRMED HER AS THE MOST POPULAR
FILM STAR ON BOTH SIDES OF THE
ATLANTIC IN THE MID 1940S.
SOME OF THE LOW-NECKED DRESSES
SHE WORE IN THE FILM WERE THOUGHT
TO BE TOO RISQUE FOR AMERICAN
AUDIENCES AND SEVERAL SCENES
HAD TO BE RE-SHOT WITH HER
WEARING MORE MODEST OUTFITS.

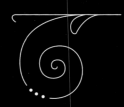

The tuppenny rush

WE HANDED OVER OUR 2D, 3D OR 4D, RUSHED TO THE BEST SEATS, SUCKED OUR GOBSTOPPERS, CHEERED THE HEROES, BOOED AT THE VILLAINS AND GENERALLY MADE A NUISANCE OF OURSELVES. FOR MOST OF US THE SATURDAY CINEMA CLUBS WERE OUR FIRST INTRODUCTION TO THE MAGIC WORLD OF THE FLICKS...

A WHITE PLASTIC ARMBAND

I N WEYMOUTH in the 1950s it seemed that the great majority of the town's children converged on the Saturday Morning Cinema Club, either at the Regent, the Odeon or the Belle Vue - known as 'The Bug 'utch'.

Which one we went to depended on which of them happened to be operating the children's cinema at the time or, if two of them were, which one gave away the best prizes, gifts or badges.

Eventually I managed to get on the committee of all of them in turn, which entitled me to wear a white plastic arm-band with the words 'Committee Member' written on it in black. This meant that, once all the queue duties had been carried out, I got free admission.

The most popular films were the cartoon and the Western, invariably starring either Roy Rogers or Gene Autry.

The least popular were those that contained any hint of romance, when the noise level of the bored audience rose to a deafening climax.

The clubs used to hold competitions for colouring-in pictures that appeared in the local newspaper, talent contests and, at the Regent, which had a large stage, team games organised by the committee members. These were held just before the serial or feature film.

However, the two most memorable events, for me, were the visit to the Odeon of 'Snowy' (or was it 'Jock'?) from Dick Barton - Special Agent, and a 3-D film at the Belle Vue where we were all issued with special glasses with one eyepiece red and the other green.

Needless to say, despite the request from the manager that all glasses be returned, the committee members managed to collect only six!

James Davis

ALONE IN MY TIP-UP SEAT

A SHORT TIME after the war ended in 1945, Saturday morning pictures for children resumed in my home town of Romford in Essex. These took place at the Havana Cinema in South Street and I usually went with two or three friends.

One morning I joined the noisy queue of children waiting to go in, but when the doors opened I found that my friends had not come as usual, so I did not know whether to go in or not.

While I was still making up my mind, I was swept along with the seething crowd into the dimly-lit cinema where I sat quiet and alone in my tip-up seat, while all around me children shouted, waved, ate apples, and dropped sweet papers. A cheer went up as the elegantly-draped curtains parted and the films began.

I tried to be interested in the adventures of The Prisoner of Zenda and the Perils of Pauline but without my friends it was just not the same. The last straw was the obligatory Western, which I always hated, so without even waiting for my favourite cartoons, I got up from my seat and made my way back into the silent foyer.

Glossy black and white still photographs of favourite film stars lined the walls. Veronica Lake looked over her shoulder at me from behind her peek-a-boo page-boy hairstyle.

The cinema manager emerged from his office hidden behind felt-lined walls. He barred my way, surprise written on his face. "Where are you going, little lady?" he asked.

"Home. I don't like it." I replied primly.

Looking puzzled, he allowed me to pass through the heavy glass doors and out into the glaring sunshine.

Was I the only child ever to walk out of the Saturday morning pictures?

Audrey Confrey

IT WASN'T ME!

ONE OF my most bitter, but comic, memories of old-time movie shows in Cambridge was being frog-marched in disgrace out of the Kinema Cinema in Mill Road.

It happened in about 1925 at a Saturday afternoon children's programme showing at the 'Fleapit', as the Kinema was affectionately known. The film show featured my favourite cowboy, Tom Mix.

I was ushered right down the front to the first row seats, nick-named the 'neckbreakers'.

In front of me was a long brass pole from which hung a red velvet curtain to hide the musicians, who were also watching the film so they could play the appropriate music.

I had been sitting there for only about five minutes when an usher came down, shone a torch, grabbed me by the neck, marched me outside and dared me to go in again.

Non-plussed, I asked him why. He told me that a boy had been taken short and relieved himself over the curtain on to the man playing the drums.

It was no good me protesting that it was the boy in the next seat. The usher was convinced it was me.

Graham Richardson

IN COUNTRY districts there was often little or no entertainment, so if there was a cinema, we were very lucky.

Our mothers, many of whom were war widows, usually managed to conjure up the magic coppers so we could go to the pictures. The lowest price was 4d.

The fourpennies were un-upholstered benches at the front of the cinema. As many of us as possible crowded ourselves on to the benches farthest from the screen, those at the end of the row clinging on for dear life.

From there, before the performance began, we watched the more fortunate passing by to the cushioned comfort of the ninepennies, or the incredible luxury of the one and twos.

Sometimes we hadn't got 4d, but would still gather outside the cinema, if only to gaze enviously at those who did go in.

The manager, often standing at the door for the first performance, would tell us to hurry along if we were coming in.

"We can't," was our pathetic reply. "We haven't got the money today." At the same time we eyed him hopefully. Then a pause as he looked at us. "Well, get inside quickly," he'd say. "And mind you, no noise. You'll help keep the draught off them that can pay."

Tom Mix was our favourite, no better cowboy could personify the heroes of that great western writer, Zane Grey. Then there was the daring Pearl White, and the antics of our comedians - Charlie Chaplin, Harold Lloyd, Laurel and Hardy, and all those Mack Sennett comedy men.

But Tom Mix was also an example to us. His high moral tone made a strong impression. He never drank, smoked or used vulgarity. Impeccable in his conduct, he did kiss the girl in a few films, but we forgave him for that!

Our greatest joy was the weekly serials. How the fourpennies gaped and gasped at that melodrama, suffering the hero's hurts and rejoicing at the villain's.

How the occupants of those benches rocked from side to side as the fighting reached its climax, or the feet stamped the bare boards in unison with the galloping horses.

Meanwhile the pianist, hidden behind the brass rail and red curtaining, frantically hammered out the Light Cavalry.

And when the hero on his horse, after racing neck-to-neck with the villain, struck the final blow for cowboy justice, those on the benches could contain themselves no longer, but rose to their feet and let out a cheer that fairly rattled that old cinema roof.

Those at the end of the row, unable to maintain their precarious hold any longer, finished up sprawling in the gangway. Here, the proprietor, justly conscious of his better-paying patrons, would come in with a warning to keep quiet or be sent home.

In those days the heroes always came through in the end and the villains always received their just deserts. The films taught us children there was a right and wrong, and that crime was never intended to pay, or to be excused.

J.H. Hook

THE THRUPENNY RUSH

At two o'clock on a Saturday
Not a kid on the streets could be seen,
We'd all be 'down the bug 'ouse',
Gazing up at the silver screen.

We used to call it the thrupenny rush,
No prizes for guessing why;
Scores of kids, pushing and shoving,
Shouting - some would even cry.

It's a wonder that man who opened the doors
Wasn't trampled to death in the crush,
As we all charged into the foyer,
Where a frightened old lady screamed 'shush!'.

After we'd paid for our tickets,
We would fight our way to the seats;
Some of them had the springs hanging out,
And some were all sticky from sweets.

When the lights went down
We'd all yell 'booray'
And the old lady again shouted 'shush'.
Then the picture began
And for two minutes, say,
There would be a wonderful hush.

But not for long,
Something always went wrong,
The sound, or the film would break down,
Then all hell would break out,
We would all scream and shout,
And the old lady's 'shush' we would drown.

The film would re-start,
And silence would reign,
As we all settled down,
In our seats once again.

Then at half past three,
Or a quarter to four,
The old lady and man
Would stand by the door
Preparing themselves for the coming stampede,
As dozens of kids slipped off the lead.

The going out was as bad as
the coming in,
You've never heard such a terrible din;
But for us kids,
There was nothing so lush,
As going 'down the bug 'ouse'
For the thrupenny rush.

David Luton

ABOVE: THE 'COLLY' - THE ELECTRIC COLISEUM AT WATFORD

REWARD FOR CLEANING UP

I REMEMBER SEEING one film, starring cowboy actor Hoot Gibson, which started off as a silent then, halfway through, became a talkie. The talkie era must have begun when the film was in production.

As with most kids of my generation my earliest cinema visits were to the tuppenny rush on Saturday mornings. The cinema was the Electric Coliseum at Watford, the town's flea pit.

On Saturday mornings, long before the performance was due to start, a queue of diminutive film fans formed along the side of the cinema.

The incentive for early arrival was the chief cleaner's (he was also the commissionaire) invitation to assist in cleaning the auditorium. The payment for this chore was a bar of chocolate (value 2d) and a free seat for the show.

The cigarette packets, chocolate wrappings and so on removed from the auditorium were deposited on a rubbish heap beside the cinema.

We often scavenged through the rubbish tip looking for pieces of film. When the film broke, as it often did at the 'Colly', the projectionist would splice the ends together, discarding in the process a few frames which found their way onto the tip. These were sought after by youngsters to be looked at through a viewer which was on sale in toy shops.

George Lorimer

9

FATTY ARBUCKLE AND COWBOY FILMS

ON SATURDAY mornings we paid 3d to see films like The Ghost Train with Will Hay, Moore Marriott and Fatty Arbuckle and cowboy films with Gene Autry and Hopalong Cassidy. But the best was the weekly serial - Zorro, Flash Gordon or The Jungle Princess among others.

Another 1d bought sweets to eat while you watched - gobstoppers and liquorice skipping rope.

It was sometimes noisy, the usherettes shone their torches on us and threatened to turn us out if we didn't behave, but there was no real trouble, just a lot of boys and girls enjoying themselves.

Joan Jackett-Simpson

LETTING OFF STEAM

THE SATURDAY matinees are still strong in my memory. First was the anxiety of raising the 'wind', as we called it, for the admission money - 2d or 3d, according to one's social standing.

We had to work for it in those days. The return of the mineral-water bottles or jam jars was a good alternative to some of the unpleasant tasks thought up for us by adults.

We received full value for our money. The bill of fare usually included a newsreel, a cartoon, a serial and the adult film currently showing in the evening performances.

In the 1930s, the glamorous events on the screen were in sharp contrast to the drab and harsh economic realities that faced us when we left to go home, but some of the magic remained with us, often to be replayed in our games.

A local character at our favourite cinema was an attendant we all called Owd Russell. I can still, in my mind's eye, see his shabby gold-braided uniform and skewed peaked hat. Benny Hill must have modelled his famous commissionaire on him!

He plodded around the theatre fighting a constantly losing battle with about 200 unruly kids. On one notable occasion a practical joker friend of mine put a 'Dirty Fido' - a passable imitation made of plaster of a domestic animal's dropping - on a seat. He beckoned Owd Russell over and pointed out this heinous offence.

Russell ruminated for a while, then suddenly seized the cinema cat who was innocently sleeping nearby. With a cry of, "You dirty b****r!" he propelled the startled animal forcibly up the aisle.

Our mirth had not subsided when he returned with a brush and shovel. Then the miracle happened! On realising it was a hoax, a slow smile crept over his face, the only time in living memory that this phenomenon had occurred.

A short time afterwards he ambled on to the stage to deal with a wisp of smoke caused by a thrown firework. He attempted to throw the contents of a fire bucket onto the smoking paper, but the water had frozen solid. His double-take was worthy of Oliver Hardy, which prompted the young audience to howls of laughter. He retreated with purpling face and threatening fist. That was more like the real Owd Russell!

The serials were the most discussed part of the programmes. We acted the previous Saturday's episode over and over through the week and made suggestions as to how the hero/heroine would escape the life-threatening situation at the end of each episode.

Next Saturday would confound all our ingenious theories, as the solutions always seem to be written by the 'in one bound he was free' school of scriptwriting. This was invariably greeted by cries of derision, but we never learned and more wild theories were still propounded the following week.

Looking back, I suppose the main feature films were totally unsuitable for our age. We watched horror films, and romantic ones, although these were far less explicit than they are today. Any suggestion of romance was greeted with inattentive chatter and the ultimate sin of a screen kiss earned itself a chorus of raspberries.

Audience participation was a phrase unknown then, but we participated all right. Loud cheers for the cartoons, cries of "behind you!" when appropriate and groans for a bumbled reel change.

It was all great fun if a little undisciplined and I suppose it allowed us to let off a little steam in a harmless way.

Alan Waterworth

MEMBER OF THE COMMITTEE

WHEN I was a teenager (50 years ago) my Saturday mornings revolved around the Cinema Club. At one point I was the holder of three membership cards - the Ritz ABC, the Odeon and one for the cinema at the bottom of my road, which had once been privately owned by the same lady who played the piano there for silent films.

At the Odeon we not only watched films and serials but ran charitable events such as collecting toys for a mother and baby home, talent competitions and floral competitions too.

One day volunteers were requested to form a committee - needless to say I joined. Every so often we climbed the curved stairs lined by the glamorous portraits of the stars to the small door of

the manager's office, and had a visit to the projection room.

We also formed a roped-off cordon outside for safety reasons to stop any children running into the road nearby.

Between 1954 and 1964 I met real film stars as a member of Sir Malcolm Sargent's Royal Choral Society. Among them were John Mills with his wife Mary Hayley Bell, Margaret Lockwood and Trevor Howard and, on a visit to Copenhagen, I once saw Rosalind Russell.

Evelyn Burr

BATMAN FOR THE REST OF THE WEEK

ONCE INSIDE the cinema on Saturday mornings, we were not quite under the control of 'Blood Pressure' - everyone's name for the poor old man who kept an eye on us. Although in those days everyone over the age of 40 looked old, I think Blood Pressure really was old.

He was actually our next-door neighbour, but on Saturday mornings we threw things at him.

While we waited for the films to start, a cheery warm-up man kept us entertained with a sing-song. All that I can remember of his repertoire are two verses of the Tale of Cecil's Whiskers:

When Cecil goes out flying, no aeroplane has he,
He uses his whiskers where the aeroplane should be.

Chorus:
Oh, they're always in the way, they're always in the way,
They hide the dirt on Cecil's shirt, they're always in the way!

*When Cecil goes out swimming, no
swimming trunks has he,
He uses his whiskers where the swimming trunks should be.*

I think we used to make up a few
verses ourselves, which I don't think
was too difficult!

In those days you knew where you
were - the villains were real villains and
the heroes were real heroes.

Later, when we got home, a few minutes with some black cloth, a pair of
scissors and some thread and we had a
mask. All we had to do then was sling
our raincoats over our shoulders, do up
the top button, and we were Batman
for the rest of the week. It was usually
far too cold to be Tarzan!

Chris O'Donoghue

WE ALL STOOD TO ATTENTION

*Two seats in the back row,
For only one and six.
And for tuppence on a Saturday,
Tom Maynard and Tom Mix.*

*It's true we were a rowdy lot,
We'd shout and stamp and sing.
But - we all stood to attention,
When they played God Save The King!*

Gerry Boxall

DARING BLACK ACE

THE BLACK ACE, as I recall from
Saturday morning matinees, was
a daring fighter pilot. Dressed
entirely in black, he was forever saying
into his microphone, "Black Ace calling,
Black Ace calling".

I can't remember what or who it was
he did call, but it always led to yet
another dangerous and heroic act.

I remember, too, that he depended a
lot on his mechanic, appropriately
named Jelly Beans because of the
enjoyment he got by throwing a jelly
bean into the air and catching it in his
mouth.

Black Ace, like all the other heroes,
had us all in a fever of excitement and
eagerly looking forward to - 'Next
week's thrilling episode'.

CH Giles

Your favourite pin-ups

✫ *Gregory Peck* ✫

(BORN 1916)

13

Handsome and likeable on screen, Gregory Peck had women's hearts fluttering from the 1940s onwards. He made his film debut in 1943 in 'Days of Glory' and a year later, in his first starring role as an ageing priest in 'The Keys of the Kingdom', he gained an Oscar nomination. Many British audiences will remember him with great affection when he starred with Audrey Hepburn in the charming romantic comedy 'Roman Holiday' in 1953.

Behind the scenes

PROJECTIONISTS, USHERETTES, MANAGERS, PERFORMERS - IT TOOK A LOT OF PEOPLE TO MAKE OUR VISITS TO THE PICTURES REALLY MEMORABLE OCCASIONS...

A CASHIER'S LIFE

IN 1942 I worked as a cashier at the West End Cinema in Suffolk Street, Birmingham. It was a large, rambling Victorian building that had been used as a theatre in the early 1900s. It still had the dressing rooms and long, winding passages behind the screen.

I always felt it was haunted on the rare occasions when I dared myself to go behind the screen, more out of curiosity than necessity. It was so dark and creepy.

In the circle there was an open restaurant where patrons could sit and enjoy a meal before or after the show. There were also side balconies where they could sit and watch the film at the same time.

When I was on my 'break', I would sit there with a glass of orange juice and watch a half-hour excerpt from the current film. I never saw the beginning or the end, unless I stayed on after I had finished cashing up.

The Gainsborough films were very popular at that time, and one of our promotions was to have the real Gainsborough Lady on stage as the film opened in a replica setting. She turned and bowed to the audience to the Gainsborough theme, as she did in the film.

It was very effective, even if she did look a lot older in real life than on film.

The American and Canadian Forces were stationed nearby and one evening Joe Louis (the Brown Bomber) came with some friends to see the film.

He paid 1s 9d for the cheapest seat. It surprised me but it seems that at that time in America the front stalls were the dearest seats.

I loved working at the West End Cinema. There was always something exciting going on. After the films had finished at night we would show the wartime propaganda documentaries at trade shows, often attended by the star who was in the actual film. I remember standing by Eric Portman one night.

Hazel Firth

A BIT PART

MRS HARLOW was a person imbued with great glamour for my sister and me. I suppose she was about forty and had come to live next door with her daughter Elizabeth, Mr Barnet (Uncle Leslie) and his elderly mother, known as Aunt Lil, to escape the bombing in London.

The whereabouts or even existence of any Mr Harlow we never did discover.

Mrs Harlow was warm, flamboyant and had red hair. She smelled of scent and had a throaty laugh.

Sometimes in the afternoon, my friend Elizabeth would say that she had been sent to us to play as her mother and Uncle Leslie were "having a lie down" upstairs.

Elizabeth was older and more sophisticated and would give me a knowing wink which I barely understood. Aunt Lil had invariably gone to the hairdressers.

Mrs Harlow had done a bit of acting. Before the war, she told us, she had had a part, with the actor Conrad Veidt, in a film called I Was a Spy - a tale of espionage in the First World War.

So, when it came to one of the two small cinemas in our town, the whole of my family trooped along to see it.

The seats were 6d for the best ones in the back stalls and 3d for the front. If you sat in the cheaper seats you had to crane your neck right back to see the screen and went home stuck in that position for hours.

Elizabeth, my sister, and I were given boxes of chocolates (someone's saved-up rations) to keep us quiet and we sat, enthralled, as the film started.

It was two-thirds over before Mrs Harlow appeared on the screen. The scene - a railway station with wounded soldiers being brought in from battle.

The camera zoomed in. A soldier lay on a stretcher on the platform. And over him bent the figure of a nun.

The nun turned and, for a second, looked up into the camera in anguish. Barely recognisable, her face enclosed in cowl and head-dress, was Mrs Harlow.

The film ended, we all trooped home in the blackout.

"Marvellous!" "Wonderful!" I could hear my elders saying.

But never again did our glamorous neighbour seem quite the same person to one impressionable ten-year-old.

Janet Tegetmeier

SHOWING YOU TO YOUR SEAT

A S AN ardent film fan from a very early age, it seemed logical, when I was in my teens, to become an usherette.

I always looked forward to the first showing of the main feature when I could enjoy the magic of the wonderful MGM musicals of the 1950s.

You were taken into a world of escapism - dancing with Gene Kelly, singing with Howard Keel or dreaming you were Doris Day.

Usually these films were shown three times a day, six days a week, but I would never tire of them.

Sundays were always devoted to the old black and white films and I remember queues all around the cinema to see Humphrey Bogart or Bette Davis, which frequently resulted in standing room only.

In those days I lived and breathed the cinema.

Irene Purslow

FILMS FOR THE YOUNGSTERS

IN 1949 my wife, five-year-old daughter Wendy and myself went to settle in Wincanton. I got myself a job with a local radio and electrical firm in the town.

I'd always been interested in photography and so joined the local camera club. Here I extended my hobby to 9.5mm amateur cinematography .

The only sound on amateur cine in those days was on the large 16mm, but in 1930, sound on 9.5mm came out.

Money was very tight in those days so it was a case of make your own. With the help of one of the electronic technicians I worked with, we built a sound head and amplifier to suit the cine projector I had. I spliced the film into a loop to save re-threading.

Our test filmstrip was of the changing of the guard in London - God Save The King we called it.

We spent months trying to get it right. What next? I made a few silent films of my own then started hiring films which I showed on the white wall in the lounge. Wendy's friends were the audience.

The news spread and people wanted to hire me and my projector for parties. My wife had the idea that I should hire the local, unused North Street School room on a Saturday and give a children's film show.

The hall would cost 2s 6d and the film hire 10s. I found out I could only charge 3d entrance as any more and I'd have to pay entertainment tax. So 3d it was.

Wendy found out what sort of films her friends would like to see - Mickey Mouse, Popeye, The Three Stooges and Tom Brown's Schooldays seemed to be the favourites.

I'll never forget that there was dead silence all the way through Tom Brown's Schooldays, where with Mickey Mouse it was a noisy lot all enjoying themselves. At one time I had 200 children in the hall.

It got so popular that I was invited to give shows in outlying villages.

Then some idiot invented TV...

Reg J Wilson

SMART IN BLUE

WHEN I WAS in my early twenties I worked as an usherette at the Lewisham Gaumont Theatre, quite a large and somewhat luxurious cinema incorporating a lovely restaurant.

The work was, at times, rather tiring and the hours were long. However, I enjoyed my spell there.

Our uniforms were blue with white trimming and looked quite smart.

While I was there I wrote a number of poems connected with this cinema. Here is the shortest one:

JUST AN USHERETTE

At different jobs I've tried my hand,
But none do I like better
Than being just an usherette
At a large Gaumont Theatre.
In uniform so trim and neat
And a torch that's nice and bright
We work most days from 2pm until
quite late at night.
Though unimportant we may seem,
This really isn't so.
If we are not on duty,
Who'd know just where to go?
And if at times we grumble
And say we're "on our knees",
Don't pay too much attention,
We try our best to please.
So spare a thought, dear public,
When to the flicks you go,
For the usherettes you meet there,
Are human too, you know.

Elsie May Phipps

I WAS 18 when I got a job as an usherette at the lovely cinema/theatre in Ealing. I took the job chiefly because my parents were strict and I had to be in at 9.30pm. Being an usherette I had shift hours of 2pm till 11pm, so I stayed out - lovely.

Before we went on duty the manager would line us up for inspection. Our green uniform was smart with quite a short skirt. The seams of our stockings had to be dead straight.

Although I wore specs usually I didn't at work - it wasn't allowed, only attractive girls were employed at the Forum.

Patrons stood along the wall inside and when a seat became empty we had to flash the first ones in the queue and then show them into the vacant seat.

When I was training - now remember I had no specs on - I showed someone a seat I thought was empty by the side of a huge fat lady.

After I'd returned to the back where we sat I hear a man's voice shout, "Where's that bloody girl, there's no seat along here!". It turned out that a little boy was already sitting in the seat next to the fat lady. I hid and another usherette calmed him down.

We usherettes in the stalls played a game. All the good-looking chaps who came in, regardless of how much they'd paid, were given a best seat in the back rows. We knew we would get a date or a chocolate bar.

On the theatre nights - called A Night With the Stars - only the six best-looking usherettes were on duty, from midnight to 3am. I always got picked.

I was in charge of the circle and it took a week of learning every seat and aisle number so that we could hand out programmes.

That night we had to wear heavy make up, have a nice hair do and wear a special uniform which had a low neckline. And, of course, we wore black stockings and black court shoes.

It was lovely. At midnight the patrons came in, all wearing evening dress, and were shown into their seats. The ceiling would open during the interval and balloons would drift down.

After the show we were taken safely home by 4am (my parents hated this night).

Eventually I became 'head girl'.

Every day at about 3pm a man would come in and sit in the back row. At about 3.30pm a fat lady came in and sat next to him. After a time he would unbutton her blouse...

The girls dared me to flash my torch on them, but I did better than that. I said, "There is a time and a place for this but this is neither the time or the place".

They didn't come in again. Wasn't I a spoil-sport?

Oh, you would never believe it, what went on when the lights went out!

Frankie Fullam

USHERETTES HAD TO BE SMART
FOR THE MANAGER'S INSPECTION

DELPHINE (INSET) AND BESIDE THE BODY OF THE 'DEAD' PRINCESS

I WAS DRACULA'S HANDMAIDEN

ONE DAY we were filming The Mummy, starring Peter Cushing and Christopher Lee, at Bray Studios. It was a bright day and the sand was warm underfoot. None of us looked very cheerful, though. This was probably because Christopher Lee was going to chop our heads off at the end of the scene.

One of my jobs as priestess was to anoint the body of the dead princess before being executed myself, to accompany her on the journey to the life hereafter.

For the English version I and half a dozen handmaidens wore green and silver stars - two each - with a diaphanous gown on top.

We shot each scene twice, slightly differently. For the Continental version we just wore the stars on our bust.

In both versions there was a long skirt made of some sort of crinkly material. All very tame by today's standards - this was 1958 - but in early Hammer films like The Mummy a lot was left to the imagination.

The expert on Egyptology made sure that everything was just right.

Before we arrived at the tomb there was a funeral procession with a sarcophagus pulled by two oxen.

When everything was ready the director called "Action!" and the oxen began to go. But not how the director intended - because the boy who had been put in charge of the oxen had given them their water before work, instead of after.

An ox drinks a lot of water, and two drink twice as much. And it has to go somewhere. It just poured out of them.

An assistant director looked one of the oxen in the eye and said, quite calmly, "Stop it!", which was about as effective as you would expect.

People ran around with buckets, but it became clear they couldn't keep up with the flow, so they waited until it stopped.

The sands of the desert were soaked. So was the tarpaulin underneath, and so was the studio floor.

We had to wait for a week until everything was dried and re-set.

Never work with children or animals, they say. But at least a child couldn't flood a studio!

Delphine Daiogane

CHANGING THE REELS

L EAVING SCHOOL at Easter 1943, an apprenticeship was out of the question as everyone was too busy on the war effort.

Eventually I found a job as a rewind boy at a local cinema, the Star in Castleford, Yorkshire. We started work at 10am and finished after the last performance, which could be any time between half past ten and eleven o'clock at night.

Our job after the last performance was to help the usherettes go round the whole cinema cleaning out the ash trays as a fire precaution. My wage was the princely sum of 14s 4d and I felt that I was rich.

The films were transported during the night so Monday morning was a hectic time sorting out the running order and transferring the film onto larger reels to fit the projector. A one-hour film would come on six small reels, each of which had to be checked for damage.

Often the programme would change midweek, so we had the same hectic mornings on Thursday as well. The last night of a particular programme was also a bit busy because, as each reel came off the projector, it had to be split back to its two original reels, and then checked and packed in tin boxes.

After the public had finally left, these boxes were carried down into the foyer for the film transport van to collect during the night.

Occasionally the film would arrive late on Monday morning, then it was not just hectic, more like sheer panic.

The firm that I worked for owned two of the four cinemas in Castleford - the New Star and The Queens. For economy we shared one copy of the Gaumont News so this had to be carried between the two cinemas every performance.

I did that job regularly on an old carrier bike. I didn't mind as the Queens had a young lady projectionist called Bessie! Actually, I did meet my first wife there, but it wasn't Bessie.

Having been a theatre, the Queens had a large back screen area which had been the stage. Every lunch time I used to arrive half an hour before I had to be at the Star.

There was an old harmonium back stage which I would play while the usherettes danced. That's how I met my wife.

I dreaded the children's matinees on Saturday afternoons. My job before the programme started was to patrol the upper circle carrying an old stool leg, brandishing it like a cudgel to keep the children in order.

They didn't take much notice, after all many of them were almost my age anyway.

I particularly remember the old musicals; they were superb films, full of music and dance. Then we had a spell of classical music films such as A Song To Remember, which was a dramatised version of the life of Frederick Chopin; Song of Russia, about the life of Tchaikovsky, and many others. These films gave me a love of all kinds of music which has stayed with me all my life.

I loved stars like Betty Grable, June Haver, Rita Hayworth, Cornel Wilde, Merle Oberon and Fred Astaire, to name just a few.

As an employee, I received two complimentary tickets each week to give away; mine of course always went to my parents who would come on Thursday evenings.

They would wait for me after the performance and we would walk home together discussing the film. One week it was a murder mystery; everyone who saw it thought the plot was too involved and had difficulty following it.

Thursday came and Mum and Dad came to see it. As we walked home my Dad said, "One thing about the film puzzled me; how come that the murderer came home soaking wet from the rain before he had even gone out!"

Next morning I checked the reels and found the reason - the reels had got mixed up and we were showing 1,2,4,3,5,6 - in that order.

I told the manager but he decided not to change it. "After all," he said, "it would be better to be consistent through the week".

Once we showed a film called Sahara. The main poster to go across the front of the cinema came in three parts, 'Sa', 'ha' and 'ra'. Unfortunately the commissionaire, whose job included bill posting, got the parts mixed up, and for a week we showed SARAHA!

Being 1943, there was still the occasional air raid warning. It was also my job then to go onto the side of the stage and switch on a red light as a warning.

There was also the matter of crawling under the stage to open and close the hand-operated curtains across the screen. That job was sometimes a real trial if the River Aire was well above its normal level and flooding the lowest part of the building.

When VE day eventually came, we dressed the whole front of the building in bunting and flags and had a big staff party.

We did get one day off each week, and what did we do - we went to another cinema!

I worked in the same cinema for ten years, except for my two years national service.

Louis Forster

RUNNING OUT OF ICE-CREAM

T O MOST people the manager was someone in a dinner suit who stood in the foyer greeting people as they arrived and left. In reality he had a wide range of responsibilities - I know, I was one.

Part of the job was to publicise each film and then judge how successful it would be before ordering the weekly delivery of crisps, ices and drinks. Ordering was done a week in advance so a degree of intuition was required.

We ran Chitty Chitty Bang Bang for a week while the schools were on holiday for Easter. Several weeks beforehand I started a painting competition with the help of the local schools. I provided drawings of a scene from the film to be coloured in and returned for display in the foyer prior to judging.

Demand was so great that prizes had to be offered for different age groups. Group winners got one month's free admission and the overall winner three months.

On the Wednesday we ran a matinee in the afternoon during a heavy snow storm. We filled every seat in the hall even though children were coming in with about an inch of snow on their heads.

On this occasion my wife helped as an extra usherette while my daughter, who had just started school, did her bit by ferrying fresh supplies of ices to the sales girls. The same thing was repeated on the Saturday, happily without the snow.

During that week we set a record for admissions and sales that will never be broken as the cinema is now a snooker club.

Bill Cowan

LOVELY DAYS

A GROUP OF US IN OUR UNIFORM AT THE MAJESTIC, LATER THE ABC

I ALWAYS worked in the cinema and theatre. I enjoyed it very much and didn't mind working nights.

We started at 5pm on Sundays, weekdays 1pm. We got one day off and one early night off at eight o'clock - when we went dancing in the Red Lion.

For special pictures the men on the staff were dressed in costume and stood outside. We had a large staff - a manager, assistant manager, secretary, ice cream boy, choc and cig girl - five men and seven girls.

They were lovely days; sadly it all changed when the Second World War broke out.

Marion Browne

JOYCE, JEAN, PAT AND MYSELF WHEN WE WORKED AT THE REGAL CINEMA IN HOUNSLOW

BLACKING OUT THE CINEMA

WHEN I was 15 I got a job in the projection room of our local Embassy Cinema - an unusual thing for a girl in those days.

The advertisement had been flashed up on the screen and my parents suggested I apply for it as I had several months to go before I started training as a nursery nurse at Dr Barnado's.

As the junior, my mornings were taken up with cleaning the projection room area, which included scrubbing the floor on my hands and knees.

I learned how to prime and load the machines prior to filming. On one momentous occasion I managed to black out the cinema by not switching the machines over quickly enough. A few boos drifted up from below; however, all was quickly restored to order.

One had to watch the top corner of the film for the dots which indicated the ending of a reel.

It was also my job to rewind the films after each showing, running them through my fingers and cutting and mending any tears. I always missed part of the films while thus engaged.

The music played in the interval was records supplied by a local shop. We used to put on our favourites.

I was allowed a free ticket each week which my sister enjoyed using. I didn't wish to watch films on my day off.

One film I remember particularly during that time was The Dancing Years by Ivor Novello. I got to know the songs really well by hearing them so frequently.

Rosemary Beeney

IN THE SPOTLIGHT

I LIVED in Harrow and when I left school in 1935 at the age of 14, I managed to get a job in a newly-opened cinema.

The job was fourth operator in the projection room which meant long hours and low wages, but I liked it.

In those days there was a half-an-hour stage show between films and I was soon put to work on the spotlight.

One day I was focused on the singer-dancer who was performing Top Hat. I turned away for a second and the performer danced out of the spotlight.

Pandemonium reigned. It was as though I had stolen the crown jewels. I was hauled in front of the manager and got a right old ticking off.

But to my relief I was given another chance.

Frank Farnborough

A FEAST OF GREAT ARTISTES

I WAS an usherette at the Princess Cinema opposite the Hotel Metropole in Blackpool. Then I was promoted to second cashier; now that was a joy.

Norman Evans (the Over the Garden Wall comedian) was a regular patron, he would buy three 3s 6d seats in the balcony, pay with a £1 note and tell me to keep the change. The comedian Ben Warris was also a regular.

When Mae West came to Blackpool in her show Diamond Lil, one of the actors in the show refused to pay and wanted a complimentary ticket - which he did not get. He stormed out.

I, however, enjoyed going to see Diamond Lil. Mae West was just as she was on the screen.

On one occasion when we were showing for the first time a film with Anna Neagle and Michael Wilding, I answered the phone in the cash desk. A man's voice asked how the film was going, I said it was doing well. He thanked me and said that he was Herbert Wilcox.

Blackpool then was a feast of great artistes. My favourite (and I paid 10s 6d for a balcony seat to see her) was

Jeanette MacDonald at the Opera House in 1947. I still have the programme.

Florence Brown

BETTE DAVIS looked at me with those famous piercing blue eyes, then asked, "Would you like to see my new English cottage?"

I was a film magazine editor and I was talking to her on the set of Watcher in the Woods at Pinewood Studios. "C'mon I'll take you to it," she said.

Having finished filming for the day she walked me off the soundstage to a black limo outside. Bette ushered me into the back seat and then she sat next to her driver. We drove off.

A few yards later we suddenly stopped. "We're here," she rasped in her unmistakable voice. But we hadn't even left the studio grounds!

The diminutive legendary star then walked me on to another giant soundstage. In the middle of it was the interior set of an English cottage. "There it is," she beamed. "Isn't it just wonderful? I'll be filming on it in the morning."

Any ideas of a scoop story, 'Bette Davis Buys English Cottage', quickly vanished, but I did get a fascinating interview with her when we sat alone together in her portable trailer dressing room which had been parked right next to the cottage set.

This is just one of the many happy memories I have of interviewing stars during my long association with the film magazine, Photoplay, which I edited between 1963 and 1983, and again between 1987 and 1991.

I can vividly recall sitting with John Wayne in the office of the managing director of Shepperton Studios while Big John watched a Ladies Wimbledon Final on a TV screen.

He became so involved in it that he would only answer my questions during the breaks between games. "Wimbledon," he said. "It's all about having tea and crumpets, is it?"

"No," I smiled. "It's actually strawberries and cream!"

"Oh yeh," he drawled.

On another occasion at Shepperton during the filming of The Grass Is Greener, Cary Grant suddenly asked me to open a cupboard drawer in his dressing room where I'd find a telegram he'd just received.

"Read it," said Cary.

It had been sent by Universal Studios in Hollywood informing Cary that Operation Petticoat, the submarine comedy he made with Tony Curtis, had just become the studio's greatest hit.

"No," said Cary as I quietly scanned across the words. "I want you to read it out ALOUD!"

Even the great stars of movies needed to hear things like that, for so many suffered from insecurity despite their enormous fame. Marilyn Monroe was plagued by self-doubt and insecurity. She often baffled her friends and colleagues by doing the unexpected.

While she was working on the film, Let's Make Love, which took our own Frankie Vaughan to Hollywood to co-star with her, I experienced one of Marilyn's unexpected moments.

Frankie's agent in London arranged for a small group of us to talk to Frankie on the long-distance phone. We were told there was no chance that Marilyn would talk to any of us. She wasn't doing interviews.

As the phone was passed to me after other journalists had talked to Frankie, the phone went dead. Nobody seemed to be there and then suddenly a woman's voice came on the line.

"That's not Frankie," I said. "Who's this?".

"Marilyn," came the reply. "Marilyn Monroe. What would you like to know?"

She had decided to talk to one of us.

And I was the lucky one! I almost fell off the chair and was totally unprepared to talk to the great one herself.

But those five minutes with MM will always be remembered, and so will be my meetings with Fred Astaire and Gene Kelly on a memorable May day at the Savoy Hotel in London; my two encounters with Robert Mitchum, the interviewer's nightmare who, when I asked how he kept fit, replied nonchalantly, "I lay down a lot!"

And with Richard Burton who told me his pet name for Elizabeth Taylor was Snapshot because of the attention she attracted.

Looking back over the years I can't help thinking how lucky I've been to have met so many of my own favourite stars.

Ken Ferguson

SHEER HEAVEN

I LIVED in Kent and left school in 1933 aged thirteen. It was the golden age of Hollywood and I was besotted by all the stars - Garbo, Harlow, Hepburn, Lombard etc. My first favourites were Constance Bennett and Ronald Colman.

What joy when I took a job as an usherette at a cinema called the Troc. Being able to watch films all day long was sheer heaven!

I worshipped the great Fred Astaire and when we were showing Top Hat in 1935 I never took my tea-breaks nor my early nights as I couldn't drag myself away from the screen.

I started scrapbooks of Fred. I have hundreds of photographs and articles

and all of his 78 rpm records. I wrote to him many times and once had a handwritten reply on his own notepaper which, though now fading with age, is framed and still hanging on my bedroom wall.

In 1936 when I was 16 I became cashier at a newly-built super cinema - the Oxford at Whitstable.

I shall never forget those Saturday matinees when all the kids dashed in hurling grubby pennies at me!

Joan E Harvey

ABOVE: THE OXFORD STAFF, FROM LEFT, KATH, LILY, BETTY AND JOAN

LEFT: THE OXFORD IN WHITSTABLE IN 1936

MISSING THE CUE SPOT

A S A naive 15-year-old youth I started work as a projection boy in a South London cinema. It was not my first job, but it had to be better than working in a factory.

Any ideas that I had about becoming a new J Arthur Rank were quickly dispelled!

The hours were horrendous and I was expected to do everything from making the tea to lacing up and running two huge 35mm projectors, check and repair the films, travel to another nearby movie house to collect and return a shared newsreel. If I had any time left, I had to sweep up and wash cups and plates used by the rest of the projection room staff. But it was an experience I would not have missed.

The year was 1944 and I had picked a bad time to become a movie mogul. Flying bombs were landing and one of my extra chores was to stand on the roof and keep an eye open for wayward doodlebugs.

Any readers who lived in the London area at this time will remember only too well that by the autumn of that year the bombs were raining down about one every fifteen minutes.

It was an odd thing that during the Blitz people still went to the cinema, but were reluctant to go to the movies with the flying bombs falling, so we were showing films to half empty houses.

Most of the male staff were men past the age for military service, or young sprogs like myself, but we did our best to keep things going.

The movie house was no flea pit; it was part of the ABC chain and the supreme commander was our manager. I lived in dread of 'El Supremo'.

The manager was master of all he surveyed, and he struck terror into all of the staff. I was to come under his tongue lashing often during my time in the job.

One of my most frequent offences was the 'change over'. When operating the projector you had to watch for the cue dot at the end of each reel before changing over to the second machine for the next reel. Even veteran projectionists had been known to miss it, but I made it into an art form.

The cue dot was a small white spot in the right-hand corner of the screen. Although I would try my hardest to spot it, most times I would realise too late.

Missing the signal triggered off a chain reaction, for the leader film with numbers on it would show on the screen. This resulted in the patrons in the cheaper seats at the front letting out a chorus of catcalls and whistles that would be heard by El Supremo in the foyer.

The manager would phone the projection box, and tell the chief projectionist to have the culprit report to his office.

My despair came to an end with the help of an old-timer who told me that instead of watching for the cue spot, I should watch for the last scene on the reel.

I did this and it was like being born again. I never missed another changeover, but in my eagerness sometimes a crucial part of a scene would be missed!

It was part of my job to collect a shared newsreel from another nearby cinema. I would travel there by tram (fares paid) and one terrible day I left the newsreel on the tram. I did not realise what had happened until the chief projectionist asked me where the film was.

For the moment I was rooted to the spot, then I toyed briefly with ideas of joining the Foreign Legion. When I eventually went to see the manager he gave a wonderful impression of Captain Mainwaring in Dad's Army when he said "You stupid boy!".

The lost newsreel was returned to the cinema by the tram company, but in the meantime World War Two had to go on hold.

There were many other pitfalls to the job, such as checking the films for breaks. The 800-foot reels had to be checked by hand and woebetide me if I missed a break and the show broke down. The usual weekly movie was all right because the prints were new, but the old Sunday films were often falling to bits.

To add to my misery a certain Mr Hitler was spending all day trying to demolish my place of work. I would watch from the roof as the flying bombs came over. At 15 you don't really understand fear, but I would hold my breath when the motor cut out near us.

It was not until many years later that I realised I needn't have taken all the stick from our manager, for projection boys (good or bad) were hard to come by, as a lad at that time could earn better money in a war factory.

I woke up one morning and decided that show business was not for me - J Arthur Rank would have to carry on without yours truly.

Peter Street

YOU MUST BE JOKING!

THE NEXT time the film One Million Years BC turns up on television take a look at the girls. Every one of them is wearing false eyelashes. Prehistoric? You must be joking!

This is just one glaring example of the blunders movie makers keep on perpetrating and it's worth looking out for them whenever old films are revived on the small screen.

Many mistakes are caused by directors either forgetting the period in which a story is set - or just being plain careless.

An extra in The Viking Queen can be seen wearing a wristwatch. Playing King Arthur in the film Camelot, star Richard Harris has a strip of Elastoplast on his neck.

A British comedy, The Wrong Box, was funnier than intended - as it featured television aerials sprouting on the roofs of Victorian London. And in Gone With The Wind, Vivien Leigh runs past a street-lamp lit, 20 years before its time, by electricity.

In a thriller The Verdict, set in 1890, a bare-shouldered showgirl orders playboy Peter Lorre: "Zip me up". Lorre duly obliges - which is very clever considering that zips were not invented until 1913, and the word itself not coined until 13 years later.

The same film sees Sydney Greenstreet asking a cabbie to take him to Newgate Prison - and finishing up at Scotland Yard.

Clothes worn by the stars have caused a lot of trouble. Actresses have a habit, for instance, of wearing different shoes in the same scene.

When Kathleen Turner leaps from a rooftop onto a train in The Jewel of the Nile she is wearing canvas slip-ons. As she stumbles and falls, clinging to the side of the train, her footwear consists of a pair of leather openwork sandals. When she is rescued and struggles to her feet, she is wearing slip-ons again.

You would think that Kathleen - or any woman, for that matter - would notice a howler like that. Yet take a look at Mexican actress Katy Jurado standing in a doorway talking to cattle baron Spencer Tracy in Broken Lance, a Western.

There's nothing wrong with the dialogue. But Katy's dress is a real mess - changing colour in alternate shots. How come she didn't realise the mix-up?

And here's Lee Remick, wearing a dress in a cafe scene in Anatomy of a Murder - but in slacks when she walks outside. Nor must we forget Marilyn Monroe in Gentlemen Prefer Blondes, rising from her table in a brown dress and then appearing on the dance-floor in blue.

Even that great perfectionist Katharine Hepburn manages, in the course of His Other Woman - in which she plays a researcher about to be replaced by a computer - leaving her office with a bunch of white flowers that turn pink by the time she reaches the pavement.

Males stars have been just as slipshod. During one of his many screen fist fights, the old pro John Wayne lost his toupee. But seconds later it's back on his head. The film is North To Alaska.

That wasn't Wayne's only blooper. As a Western diplomat in Japan in the movie The Barbarian and the Geisha, he talks to actor Sam Jaffe - playing a character named Henry - and calls him Sam.

In the Anderson Tapes, Sean Connery and Martin Balsam achieve the impossible by drinking out of empty tea-cups.

A brief shot in 48 Hours reveals Eddie Murphy sitting with one hand beside him and the other on the back of his car seat. Rather uncomfortable, as he is supposed to be wearing handcuffs at the time.

An old favourite regularly revived on television is The Invisible Man, in which the central character, played by Claude Rains, escapes from the police.

Though he cannot be seen, he is given away by his footprints in the snow. The prints are of shoes, which is unfortunate as Rains was naked when he went on the run.

Things also go wrong when real life intrudes on a film. During Judy Garland's famous performance of The Trolley Song in Meet Me In St Louis, you can hear a voice on the soundtrack calling out, "Hi Judy!"

It was probably a friend who had just turned up on the set and thought the star was still rehearsing.

John Wayne again must take the blame for bloopers in The Alamo, which he directed. In the battle sequences, mobile trailers used by the film people can be clearly seen - not to mention the mattress on which a falling stunt-man lands.

Mirrors are also dangerous for film-makers - since they have a have a habit of reflecting movie cameras. It happens in Falling In Love, a Robert De Niro and Meryl Streep film.

Meanwhile, in Stagecoach, one of the most admired Westerns of all time, it's worth looking out for the rubber tyre tracks during the Red Indian chase across the salt flats.

In Knock On Wood, comedian Danny Kaye plays an American ventriloquist chased by crooks for plans hidden in his dummies.

The cars in the London street scenes are particularly funny. They're all left-hand drive.

There's a similar mix-up in another Kaye movie, Merry Andrew, in which he plays a timid British school teacher who meets up with a bunch of circus folk.

One scene features a London bus being driven along the right-hand side of the road - with nobody bothering to object.

People in charge of movie props keep on getting careless. In Tea and Sympathy a pair of china dogs are back to back in long-shot but face to face in close-up.

Viewers of Hanover Square, a thriller about a murderous composer, are told that the story is set in 1899. How come then, that the continuity girl failed to notice a theatre programme dated 1903?

And when choosing a newspaper for Triple Cross, a World War II movie, you'd think someone would have picked one without a headline about the rising cost of Concorde - built 30 years after the war.

For true mind-blowing confusion take a look at Man About The House, a British movie in which a character is seen hailing a taxi outside the Thames TV studio - and asks the driver to take him to Thames TV.

At journey's end we watch him getting out at exactly the spot where he got in.

Only in the movies can you go to all that trouble to get nowhere!

Ivor Smullen

A BOUQUET FROM JOAN

MY DAD, Fred Grundy, used to post the advertising bills for coming attractions at the local cinemas. The posters used to come up by train to Kettering and we'd help him fold them in a special way so they were easy to stick up on the boards.

He also helped maintain the cinemas and often met the young starlets.

In 1954 the Odeon had a facelift and it was re-opened by the very young Joan Collins. The film that night was Genevieve and Joan rode through the streets in the original car used in the film.

When my mum and dad were introduced to her they told her that their little girl had been in hospital for several months.

Joan gave them her bouquet and corsage to give to me. I was so thrilled.

Patty Carroll

NOISES OFF

WHEN I was young my father, Tommy Sylvester, played the sound effects for the silent movies at the Playhouse Picture House in Pontefract where we lived at the time.

He and a pianist sat behind the screen in a darkened room.

When the epic film The Ten Commandments was being shown, each time a command was broken my father banged a door knocker which was fixed on a piece of wood. When it thundered he banged the symbols.

While they were watching the film he and the pianist could hear a sh-sh-sh sound. When the lights went up the large piece of brown paper that my father had had his symbols wrapped in had vanished through a big hole in the skirting board. It had obviously been pulled through by mice.

Pat Bryars

LONG BLACK DRESSES AND YELLOW BOWS

IN THE late 1940s my sister Barbara and I worked at the Odeon in New Street, Birmingham.

We wore long black dresses cut away to the knee with a yellow satin lining and a big yellow bow.

One day I was standing at the reception upstairs when a gentleman with his entourage walked past. I noticed he was wearing make up. He looked at me and said, "What a pretty young lady".

I was stunned when I was told it was Noel Coward.

That performance the organist played all his lovely music in the interval.

Margaret Clewley

TANGLED NEWS

I USED TO cycle between the Capitol in Upminster and the Towers cinema in Hornchurch delivering the Gaumont British News.

I wasn't allowed to go on public transport because the film was inflammable.

While cycling downhill one day I noticed a round tin rolling a few yards in front and gathering momentum. Then the lid flew off and there was my news film all over the road!

Stopping halfway down the hill I caught up with the tangled mess and spent ages rolling up the film.

At the Towers the chief projectionist was not too pleased to see the state of the scratchy film on his screen. "I'll have to get on to the Capitol and tell them their rewinding is not up to standard," he said angrily.

I never made any comment and this is the first time anyone will know what actually happened!

Richard Shelton

ROYALS IN THE CIRCLE

IN THE early years of the war I worked at the Little Theatre in Bath. Nearly every week the Ethiopian royal family, led by Haile Selassie, would arrive for an afternoon performance. He was a tiny man of immense dignity.

They were shown with great reverence to their seats by the senior member of staff. They always sat in the 1s 3d seats in the circle and never patronised the 9d stalls.

Jean Waterhouse

✫ *Myrna Loy* ✫

(1905 - 1993)

WHO WILL EVER FORGET HER AS NORA
CHARLES, THE BEAUTIFUL, WITTY WIFE
OF 'HUSBAND' DICK POWELL IN
THE THIN MAN.
MYRNA BEGAN HER CAREER AS A STAGE
DANCER. RUDOLPH VALENTINO GAVE HER
A SCREEN TEST IN 1925 AND SHE
APPEARED IN ABOUT 60 SILENT FILMS -
SHE OFTEN PLAYED A VAMP.
THE COMEDIES AND DRAMAS THAT SHE
MADE IN THE EARLY 1930S CATAPULTED
HER INTO STARDOM. IN 1946 SHE
APPEARED IN THE HIGHLY POPULAR 'THE
BEST YEARS OF OUR LIVES'.
SHE WAS A SHY STAR WHO LIVED WITH
HER MOTHER AFTER THE FAILURE OF HER
FOUR MARRIAGES.

Picture palaces

THICK CARPETS, PICTURES OF THE STARS
UP THE STAIRCASE, DEEP SEATS, RICH CURTAINS
AND SPECTACULAR LIGHTING - CINEMAS
IN THE PAST REALLY WERE PALACES.
THERE WERE THE OCCASIONAL FLEAPITS TOO!

THE PURPLE TROCADERO

WHEN I started work in 1929 my mum used to meet me with sandwiches after work and we'd often go to The Purple at Camberwell Gate. We'd pay 6d each for our seats and see two whole films. Between the films the curtain would come down and ladies would come round with a free cup of tea.

Sometimes we'd catch a tram to the Trocadero at the Elephant and Castle. Here, for 6d, we'd see two films, an hour's floor show and we also had Reginald Dixon rising up from the floor playing on the organ.

In 1943, when I was in the Land Army, I married and my husband and I went to Amen Corner at Tooting Broadway to see a Gracie Fields film. The cinema was full of soldiers and Gracie was singing "Wish me luck as you wave me good-bye".

Bill was going away the next day - it turned out I wouldn't see him again for five years.

When the lights went up I don't think there was a dry eye in the place.

R Bishop

GREENFORD'S GRANADA

I WOULD like to take you back to 1938 when the Granada at Greenford opened its doors for the first time. It was an absolutely magnificent cinema.

I was ten years old and stood outside with crowds of other people watching for the 'big star' who was to officially open the cinema. It turned out to be none other than Gracie Fields. There she was on the steps of the cinema dressed as an usherette with an 'ices for sale' tray. All the usherettes wore blue and yellow silk uniforms.

On Saturday mornings I became a Greenford Grenadier. For 6d I saw the Magic Kingdom Cartoons, The Three Stooges, the big film plus the serial - Flash Gordon.

As I got older I would go with my friends at least once a week. What value for 1s 9d - the big film, a B movie, shorts, newsreel, the great organists like Robinson Cleaver, plus stage shows such as Carrol Levis and his Discoveries, and Bryan Michie and his road show.

The cinema building is still there - but now it's a supermarket.

Bill Tofte

33

GLAMOUR IN SOUTHEND

MY CHILDHOOD was spent at Hadleigh, near Southend, and I remember the Kingsway cinema there. It was built in the 1930s and was opened by Betty Field, then a fairly famous actress.

It was a beautiful place. The cinema organ had a glass surround which kept changing colour. We used to love it as it came up from the depths. One of the organists I remember was Cedric Uron.

Sometimes when I was in my teens I went during the afternoons. Several times I had to change seats because some 'gentleman' decided that even though the cinema was nearly empty, he would come and sit next to me. They wanted to play either footsie or kneesie!

The usherettes used to walk backwards down the aisle squirting smelly stuff, presumably scented disinfectant.

The Odeon at Southend was a real palace and had a lovely restaurant where we used to eat sometimes when we went straight to the pictures from work in London.

Sometimes a crowd of us from the club I belonged to went to the pictures on a Sunday evening. Two would queue up for the tickets and the rest would wait inside.

The films really took us away from everyday life. The stars were very glamorous and I used to read all about them in my older sister's Picturegoer and Picture Show magazines.

Beryl M Kalsey

OUR LOCAL VILLAGE HALL

WHEN A local village hall started showing films once a week, my mother and I, both ardent film-goers, decided to go. It was a lot cheaper to get in and there were no bus fares to get there.

There was a lovely community spirit there, everyone knew everyone else and people of all ages joined in.

The first film I saw there was Annie Get Your Gun. I remember the projector kept breaking down and the shouts of "Boo!" from the lads in the back row.

Toffee papers were thrown around and there was a lot of larking about in general.

We didn't really win because the seats were so uncomfortable we had to take our own cushions. We went back to the comfort of the cinema again.

Maureen Pearce-Webb

KINEMA IN THE WOODS

THE FIRST cinema I remember is the Kinema in the Woods at Woodhall Spa in Lincolnshire. I spent several childhood years in this small town and my sister, two brothers and I loved to go to this cinema.

We stood on a form at the back and, later on, when we graduated to the front seats, which were deck-chairs, we felt very grand!

Dorothy Birkbeck

FRIDAY NIGHT AT BRUCE GROVE

WHEN I was a child living in Tottenham, North London, we had at least three cinemas close by. But the one we went to most was the Bruce Grove Cinema.

We used to queue for the 1s 6d stalls down a side alley that led to the car park. It was never crowded as very few people had cars in the 1940s and 50s.

When we got in the building we walked down a sloping floor to the box office to get our tickets.

Further along the street was a grander entrance with steps leading up to it where you got tickets for the upper stalls or, if you were more affluent, the balcony.

Mum usually took my sister and me to the pictures on Friday nights. On the way home we would all have a three-penny bag of chips and walk along discussing the film.

J Rosser

SILENCE IS GOLDEN

IN THE early 1930s, when I was quite young, I had a job in which I shared the limelight, in a sense, with celebrities. The rewards were great and I basked in the adulation of my public. It was heaven but it could not last...

Tredegar, a South Wales valley town, had three cinemas: the Workmen's Hall, the Market Hall and the Queen's, all showing silent films in two separate programmes per week.

The Market Hall was considered rather posh because it sported a balcony and as the seats were priced at 9d,

1s and 1s 3d, it was rarely frequented by the 'hoi-polloi'. It showed classic films, four-reelers like Birth of a Nation or Orphans of the Storm, almost as soon as they were made.

The programme, usually the feature film and one 'short', was always accompanied by the cinema pianist perched at his battered old upright just below the screen. The middle and upper classes of the town came here to be entranced by the performances of Mary Pickford, Douglas Fairbanks and the Gish sisters.

The Workmen's Hall, more reasonably priced at 6d, 9d and 1s, attracted the bulk of the working class. Here you would see the occasional classic film but months, or sometimes years, after it had been shown at the Market Hall.

Film stars such as Blanche White, Bessie Love and Conrad Veidt made regular appearances, generally in two-reelers. Mary Pickford's Pollyanna and Poor Little Rich Girl were shown, but years out of date, as were Mark of Zorro and The Gaucho in which her husband Douglas Fairbanks featured.

The programme was usually made up of several films and occasionally on Saturdays there was a piano accompaniment.

Compared with these two the Queen's was a veritable fleapit. Customers sat on hard wooden seats in a dingy hall that had probably never been redecorated. But, being the cheapest cinema in town, it had a band of faithful fans who loved the programmes, usually one-reelers with the main event of the evening being the serial.

One episode of films like Song of Songs or The Wandering Jew would be shown each week which meant that you would have to go regularly for about twelve weeks to see the whole film.

It was through these serials, The Fall of Troy, The Last Days of Pompeii, Custer's Last Stand and The Charge of the Light Brigade, that I learned much history. Later I learned some religion, too, from films such as The Ten Commandments and Quo Vadis.

My general knowledge was increased by being told such things as the walls of Babylon were three hundred feet high, six times the height of our town clock.

For pure entertainment I preferred the Westerns - Hoot Gibson, Buck Jones and Tim Holt became my heroes. But perhaps the most memorable films were the comedies. The slap-stick antics of Harold Lloyd or of Marie Dressler and the Keystone Cops often concluded the programme and sent everyone off home in a happy frame of mind.

The more subtle comedy of Harry Langdon, Fatty Arbuckle, Ben Turpin, Chester Conklin and Buster Keaton was appreciated just as much. But every one of these faded before the brightest star of all, Charlie Chaplin. This man was worshipped world-wide but nobody could have loved him more than I did.

My maternal grandmother took me to the pictures four times a week. On Monday night we went to the Queen's and on Tuesday to the Workmen's Hall. Then on Friday, after the change of programme, we went to the Workmen's Hall and on Saturday we were back at the Queen's. Her reason for taking me was not only for my pleasure.

I was quite a bright little boy. I had started school at three and a half, already able to read. She, like most of her cronies, had never been to school and was totally illiterate. My job was to read her the captions.

She was not stupid and could follow the plot without any help from me. But knowing the dialogue increased her enjoyment of the film. She also enjoyed the status I gave her among her friends.

I best remember our Saturday nights at the Queen's. Perched on my hard wooden seat, legs dangling and feet clear of the dusty floor, I would be surrounded by all the non-readers among my grandmother's friends.

Basking in the light reflected from the silver screen and the warmth of my ancient companions' adoration I felt as powerful as any monarch. Piled with monkey nuts, fruit and sweets it was always Christmas for me. Pampered and flattered and sprayed with the perfumed insecticide, from the hand pump that Nan and her cronies insisted the attendant aim in our direction, I began to feel I was omnipotent.

But I soon had my first lesson in practical politics: behind every king there is a king-maker. Mine was a little old woman taking great pleasure from what little she had. It was she who kept me in power.

I should have realised that my reign was coming to an end when the Market Hall was completely refurbished and reopened as the Olympia (the 'Limp' in common parlance). It was now equipped for the 'talkies' and although prices went up, the new cinema managed to attract some of the faithful away from the Queen's.

I never thought my grandmother would be tempted. But she loved Al Jolson, from his gramophone records, and when the 'Limp' put on The Jazz Singer she could not resist going to see her idol.

She enjoyed it thoroughly and a few weeks later she went to see Mammy, another Jolson film, but we continued to go to the Queen's and the Workmen's Hall.

Then the Workmen's Hall burnt down so my grandmother's visits to the 'Limp' became more frequent. Being a poor war widow she could not afford to take me. When the Workmen's Hall reopened it was as a 'talkie' picture palace charging prices that everyone could afford. I realised that my days of glory were coming to an end. The Queen's staggered on for a time but finally closed. Some said that it was because a rat had jumped on to a young woman's lap and had caused her to have a fit. But most people knew that the true reason was a catastrophic fall in attendances.

My grandmother continued to go to the cinema four times a week but all the films were now 'talkies'. She no longer had need of my services. I was redundant; thrown on the scrap heap at the age of seven!

Nan still showered me with love and kindness but nothing would ever replace the rewards and the satisfaction I gained at the old Queen's. The pain of that redundancy haunts me still.

Mervyn Prosser

NIGHTS IN NOTTINGHAM

I FIRST visited the local picture house in the mid 1940s when I was about six. My parents were friends of the manager and we had complimentary reserved seats twice a week on the front row of the balcony - luxury indeed.

My early favourites were Errol Flynn, Alice Faye, Betty Grable, Roy Rogers and the Bowery Boys. Then a new star burst onto the screen who overshadowed all the others - Doris Day.

Our visits to this picture house came to an end when it was badly damaged by fire and re-opened as a Woolworths.

I remember huge queues forming outside Nottingham's cinemas for The Jolson Story, The Greatest Show on Earth and The Robe.

I little imagined then that one day I would visit Hollywood and meet Debbie Reynolds, Troy Donahue, Stella Stevens and Tommy Kirk.

David Richmond

DREAMS AT THE STAR

IF THE Hollywood of the thirties was the world's dream factory then the Star Cinema in a Birmingham suburb was the palace where they were transformed into reality.

Here I could be transported to a jungle, a desert island, a Paris neighbourhood or wherever the studios of the day decided to take me. They were all exciting and stirred the vivid imagination of this then ten-year-old schoolboy.

Saturday afternoons at the Star were a regular feature of my existence and the sternest punishment that could be meted out was to have this visit denied (a rare occurrence thank heavens!)

Armed with sixpence which I earned on the Saturday morning, I had sufficient for a magnificent afternoon's self indulgence. My first call would be to the sweet shop where for tuppence one could spend a pleasurable half hour's anticipation of goodies to come.

My second call would be to a slim cigarette machine outside the sweet shop. I felt this was uniquely designed for errant school boys bent on nefarious intent. For one penny one could procure two Woodbines and three matches in a slim paper packet.

Magnificently equipped I made my way to the cinema or picture house as they were sometimes called. I would present my tuppence for a ticket for a magic afternoon's entertainment.

There was an added bonus when one purchased one's ticket. Six of the tickets which were to be sold on the Saturday afternoon were marked with a cross. Any lucky recipient of a ticket with a cross would be the winner of a ride in the cinema owner's black Rolls Royce.

The Rolls stood on the forecourt of the cinema and the owner, a benevolent, silver-haired Jewish gentleman, would always be there to greet his Saturday afternoon clientele. Impeccably dressed in black, adorned with gold watch and chain, he was a much revered and respected figure.

Although a regular attendant over a number of years I never won this coveted prize.

This was the era of the star system, and what stars they were! Who could forget Wallace Beery as Long John Silver in Treasure Island or Lew Ayres' untimely end in All Quiet On The Western Front or the early Humphrey Bogart and James Cagney in Angels With Dirty Faces? There was George Arliss in Voltaire and Johnny Weismuller as Tarzan the Original Ape Man. Errol Flynn and David Niven were on the brink of long careers in the film world with their appearance in Charge Of The Light Brigade.

I haven't forgotten the screen goddesses who supplied the love interest. Greta Garbo, Madelaine Carrol, Joan Crawford, Jean Harlow, Myrna Loy and Marlene Dietrich to name but a few.

The afternoon's entertainment was always rounded off with a serial. Each serial would last between ten and fifteen episodes and such was the blood-curdling content they invariably guaranteed their audience for the following week. Cleverly contrived, they always ended on a cliff-hanger.

Pandemonium reigned during the serial. Imaginations were at fever pitch and the noise was deafening. These climaxes sent me into a frenzy of excitement and I would run home like a lunatic. I couldn't understand why my mother didn't share my unbounded enthusiasm.

I had a week to calm down for yet another Saturday afternoon spent in the dream palace that was The Star.

Bob Isaac

HUDDERFIELD'S BEST

BORN AND brought up in Huddersfield, with the Regal nearby, the Waterloo a walk across some fields, and many more cinemas in the town centre, the flicks played a magical part in our young lives.

Mind you, my first-ever film was seen not at a cinema, but at another organisation that meant so much to us - the Co-op, the Co-op Victoria Hall in Huddersfield to be precise. Man of Arran was its title.

In my old diaries I have a list of films and where I saw them in the years 1937 to 1945. Captain January, starring Shirley Temple, which I saw at the Crescent in Leeds in 1937 heads the list. Out of 211 films only once did I dare set foot in the fleapit - that's the name I'm afraid we gave the Picturedrome in Huddersfield Town Centre.

At the children's Saturday morning films at the Regal we enjoyed singing as loud as we could:
"When you cross the road
by day or night
Beware of the dangers
that loom in sight.
Look to the left and look to the right
And you never ever will get run over".

Although there was very little traffic on the roads - it was a wonderful way to teach children road sense.

Geoffrey Darby

POPPING IN TO THE NEWS THEATRE

THE NEWS theatres hold very special memories for me. These small, but very comfy, cinemas were to be found in most cities during the 1930s, 40s and early 50s. Although primarily to show news items, their programmes were varied and full of interest.

You might remember that the show usually ran for one hour, although when there was a special feature they would run for longer. Many patrons slipped in during their lunch break, others in the middle of the afternoon; many would go along prior to an evening engagement. Not everyone remained for the whole programme, although most did.

Apart from up-to-the-minute news from around the world, there were travel films which revealed many lovely and exciting places with strange-sounding names.

Of course those days not many of us were able to venture abroad for their holidays, but those lovely travelogues evoked many a wistful dream. There were also fascinating aspects of other peoples' lives shown in detail, and you learned about customs and traditions you had never heard about before.

Watching the royal family was another delight, particularly if the two little princesses featured as well. There were often brief but interesting glimpses into the lives of the rich and famous; these would include the magic world of Hollywood with its larger-than-life celluloid idols.

Then there were the cartoons, always an integral part of the news theatres.

They were not to be missed. All the well-loved characters were there to entertain: Mickey Mouse, Donald Duck and dear old Goofy to name a few.

We sat back and laughed at their antics, enjoying every crazy bit, no matter what our age!

From time to time there would be a showing of a full-length Disney film and I will never forget the tears that were shed when I watched Bambi for the first time!

It was after that touching but enjoyable film that, while drying my eyes in the foyer, I bumped into an old school friend. She introduced me to her companion, the manager of the news theatre.

That turned out to be the most important news item of my life, for the gentleman was destined to become my husband, although I did not know it then!

Gloria M Sutcliffe

FLEA-HOPPING AT THE BOULEVARD

ALTHOUGH many of the cinemas of my boyhood had beautiful facades and were like palaces inside, the one I remember most was an old fleapit.

The Boulevard was notorious as a flea-hopping joint. The staff used to spray disinfectant between the rows during the performances to try and hide the smell. No wonder it ponged - on Saturday matinees many of the lads would wee in the aisle and little rivers would run down to form a pool in front of the stage below the screen.

The ladies lavatory was situated rather inconsiderately at the side of the screen. There was one poor girl who seemed to have trouble with her waterworks and needed to pay a visit four or five times during the film.

Each visit meant she had to climb the steps to the top of the stage as if going up for an award. Then, when she opened the toilet door, the light shone on her in the dark auditorium like a spotlight. A gang of rowdy youths cheered and clapped her every visit. "Hooray! There she goes again!"

The manager, a little bald-headed man, would patrol the aisles with a stick. Just hearing it thwack in the dark silenced any troublemakers for a while.

One of the most famous characters who used to frequent the Boulevard was Fearless Freddy the Flyer, so called because he used to leap over the cinema seats, often two rows at a time, and land right in the seat next to you.

He was harmless enough, but his appearance - he was cross-eyed and wore his cap pulled down to his eyebrows - along with the suddenness of his landing, meant he often frightened the living daylights out of people.

The Boulevard always seemed to be busy - perhaps because it was the cheapest flicks for miles around, or perhaps a lot of the clientele wouldn't be allowed in anywhere else.

It was also run on a shoe-string - literally! Washers were issued instead of tickets and were threaded by the usher on to a string and re-used. Also, as the paddings of the seats wore through, they weren't replaced until the seats were no more than bare boards.

Despite, or should that be because, of these cost-cutting exercises, time caught up with the Boulevard and it closed.

I decided to pay it one last visit. I could hear Fearless Freddy leaping at the back somewhere; my behind was sore from sitting on the wood which masqueraded as a seat; I got sprayed in my earhole with disinfectant and, to cap it all, I caught a flea.

Richard Moore

FEET AT THE TOP IN RYE

MY FIRST memories of the cinema go back to the 1920s when I was a boy living at Rye in Sussex. It was a small building with bench seating at the front for 6d and tip-up seats for 9d and 1s 3d.

When you entered the only lights were gas lamps over the exits. There was no electricity in Rye at that time so there was a generator situated at the rear of the building. You would hear this start up, and the lights would then slowly light up.

The manager would then close the exits and seat himself at a piano at the front of the screen.

He would signal the operator with a bell push by his side. The lights would go down, and the adverts would be shown in the form of 'slides'. They would often appear upside-down when the manager would angrily signal to the operator.

My all-time favourite actor was Tom Mix. I also like Charlie Chaplin, and Laurel and Hardy. Favourite actresses were Clara Bow (the 'It' girl) and Betty Balfour, a British girl.

The pianist would have favourite tunes for each situation.

Sometimes the film would have a line in the middle of the screen with the actors' feet at the top of the screen, and their heads at the bottom. More frantic signals to the operator! At other times the generator would stop in the middle of the show.

We even had to wait for the film to arrive by the next train at times. But we thoroughly enjoyed it all.

Fred Ramsden

LOOKING FOR DORIS DAY

DURING the 1950s the town of North Shields boasted six cinemas, three of which I believe could have been classed as excellent, one reasonable, and the other two rough, although not in violent terms - basically because of the inferior seating, and the countless posts which supported the upstairs.

It was tough luck if you got stuck behind one of the posts. You spent the entire evening straining your neck to see the film, the post stuck between your legs. Complaints to the manager, who normally looked more fed up than you were, were brushed aside, and you were told to jump into someone else's seat when they moved.

The Howard was such a place, but strangely enough, it was the 'in' place for teenagers on a Friday night. We turned up in droves in our smart gear, hair slicked down with Brylcreem. I suppose that apart from the obvious attraction - girls - the freedom to move around was a bonus.

Supervision was lax. The old lady who commanded the upstairs section was content with her knitting, while downstairs, the old man usually nodded off. And so, wandering was the order of the day.

You wandered at will, searching for your Doris Day or your Tony Curtis. If unsuccessful upstairs (1s to get in) you moved downstairs for a look, or vice-versa.

Jeering was constant as the film, normally a Boris Karloff one, repeatedly broke down. The establishment was the nearest I've ever seen to the one used in The Smallest Show on Earth, a film which starred Bill Travers and Virginia McKenna.

I only ever visited the place once on a Saturday, and wasn't at all surprised to see a chap walking around selling the Saturday night football paper. I still believe that he was ejected not because of his shouting, but because he woke up the old boy.

Sadly, the Howard was closed in 1956, and the others about the same time. They were all sadly missed.

Reg Thompson

PRIVATE CODE AT THE BOLTONS

PRE-WAR I lived in Balham, then Croydon, and spent many weekends with my uncle in Kensington. He often took me to his local cinema, The Boltons.

The Boltons, named from the Kensington road in which it stood, was patronised by quite a 'classy' audience, who understood a private code operated by the management.

Most nights the house lights went up at the end as the National Anthem was relayed through the speakers. Everyone stood firm until the end.

However, there were a few occasions (I remember two), when the lights did not go up and, before the National Anthem, there were a few quiet choruses of a Viennese waltz.

This meant Queen Mary was leaving her seat at the rear and would be in her Daimler and away while we all stood for the Anthem!

The suburban cinemas I remember best were the ABC and the Mayfair near Balham Station. Going down into Tooting there was a Classic where, for 3d, one could join a club and submit a short list of past films one wished to see. The older the film the more likely it would be chosen for re-run.

Then down to Tooting Broadway and my favourite cinema of all time, The

Granada. It was quite palatial inside and staffed by beautiful girls in yellow blouses and warm red skirts for winter and a cool royal blue for summer.

The impressive commissionaire, who marshalled the queues, wore the same colours in his uniform.

Croydon had quite a few cinemas which became my regulars. The Odeon was just a gloomy space between shops on the High Street, a corridor with a cash/ticket window in the wall halfway down, but quite decent inside. There was also the State in Thornton Heath and the Rex in Norbury, as well as the Odeon at Norwood Junction.

Then there was the wonderful Davis cinema - owned and managed by the two Davis brothers.

The Davis boasted a very large stage which allowed for several different presentations. Boxing, opera, ballet and full-size symphony orchestras and (like my favourite Granada) it had a mezzanine tea-room, with a view over the High Street.

I should also mention some other lesser cinemas which earned, or deserved, semi-affectionate nick-names like the 'bug-hutch', 'flea-pit' and ' deluxe' for fairly obvious reasons.

One such was about 50 yards along from the Granada Tooting Broadway. The seating list included 'fauteuils' at 1s. These were double seats without a dividing arm and fitted with a half-curtain on each side which - when pulled forward - gave privacy to the courting couple. Fleas often came as a bonus.

When alone, if I were watching a cowboy or a gangster movie, I would have a cap pistol in my pocket and - on the walk home - would 'shoot up' various lamp posts, hedges, pillar boxes etc.

In later years, I realised why the younger men were not keen to be saddled with a young boy who asked to be taken in as it was an A film; they wanted to sit near, or with, an unaccompanied young woman, with hopes of good times to come.

I progressed to this side of the cinema-going when I reached 15 and was often quite successful, although seeing one's conquest in full light or daylight could often be quite a shock.

Ralph Jeffery

BROUGHT TO YOUR SEAT

WHEN I was a young girl sometimes I used to stay with my aunt and uncle who lived on the Gower Peninsula in South Wales.

We used to go to the cinema at the nearby village of Penclawdd. It was a large corrugated shed and when it rained you could hardly hear the sound track.

A few yards away there was a fish and chip shop and, if you gave the usherette your money, she would pop along and get you some. You could then eat them while watching the films.

D Green

BEAUTIFUL EFFECT AT THE MARINA

A T FULWELL, in Sunderland, was The Marina, a perfect example of a small, cosy suburban cinema. It had stalls and a circle, all the seats were comfortable and upstairs at the sides were some doubles, known as the 'chummy seats', which for obvious reasons were popular with courting couples.

The Marina had a feature which I loved. This was a curtain made of a silky, translucent material which was lowered in front of the screen.

It was suspended from vertical wires about thirty inches apart, the material hanging in crescents between the wires rather like an Austrian blind.

Running the whole width of the curtain at the top and bottom and shining onto it were rows of different coloured lights which slowly revolved. The colour of the bottom of each crescent was always a contrast to that of the top; blue and gold, crimson and green, orange and purple, with all the shades in between, constantly changing.

The effect was very beautiful and relaxing and my father and I used to get there early so as not to miss the display, which ran for about five minutes before the advertisements.

Jerry Wright

LIGHTING UP THE RITZ

I WAS JUST 16 in 1936 and the Savoy cinema in Lincoln had recently opened. It had a magnificent Compton organ and, with Wilfred Southworth at the console, the first film to be shown was A Tale of Two Cities.

The interior of this magnificent cin-ema was decorated in the current style of the ABC cinema circuit of shell pink, white and pale green with seating upholstered in rose moquette.

Over the years it gave the people of Lincolnshire some of the finest talent available on its 44-foot stage.

PREVIOUS PAGE: THE RITZ IN LINCOLN AS IT WAS IN 1937. PAINTING BY STEPHEN CLARKE.

LEFT: 60 YEARS LATER

The visiting artists who used its 12 dressing rooms ranged from the Walker Brothers, Engelbert Humperdinck, the Beatles, Shirley Bassey, Tommy Steele, the Rolling Stones - the list is endless, and so are the memories.

The cinema closed in October 1988 having provided thousands of people, both young and old, with so many happy memories in the 52 years it had served the community.

The Savoy only just pipped the Ritz Cinema in the High Street by being first to open in the town for many years. This was due entirely to the Ritz having difficulties in getting some of the materials used in its construction.

I remember walking past the Ritz on the opening night, wishing I could afford the price of a seat. The entire frontage was outlined in bright red and green neon lighting, by far the most spectacular lighting in the town. The colours reflected brightly in the wet pavement and road.

Pilots reported that the lights were visible in the night sky 25 miles away over the North Sea. These were extinguished at the onset of the Second World War.

The film being shown at the opening on February 22, 1937 was San Francisco with Clark Gable and Jeanette MacDonald.

The Ritz, having survived the takeover from the Odeon circuit and a spell of closure with little change to the frontage, was bought by Brenda and Barry Stead and re-opened on February 15, 1985. They presented excellent live productions on its stage, together with some first run films, but one thing was missing. Every time I passed I looked at the structure and thought how wonderful it would be if the neon lighting was in place again.

After studying the brickwork through binoculars, and making copious notes and sketches, I made a large photocopy of the exterior and plotted the markings of the old anchor points still visible on the brickwork.

Using these I marked the lines of neon tubing in colours that I and others remember, onto the photocopy. Using this picture as a guide, my son Stephen painted a 16 by 12 inch picture in oils. When this was finished I photographed it and sent a colour print to Barry Stead as a Christmas card.

Barry used my son's painting as a guide and had the neon lighting reinstated. The Ritz exterior was wonderfully restored to almost the original state it was in at the opening in 1937.

Sadly, on Thursday, January 8, 1998, the Ritz came to an end of 60 years of screenings. The building is now set to become another public house.

On the final night Brenda and Barrie Stead treated the audience to free ice cream.

George Clarke

THE GLORIOUS REGAL

DURING THE 1920s, Camberley, our nearest town, had two cinemas. A small one called The Academy was situated opposite the gates of The Royal Military College, Sandhurst.

It was often frequented by the cadets, who all seemed to ride old bicycles. These machines would be parked or piled at the side of the cinema and I often wondered if, at the end of the show, these young men just grabbed any cycle and pedalled madly back to the College?

The second cinema, called The Arcade, was at the other end of the main London Road. You walked through an elegant arcade, with little intimate shops on either side, to the box office.

In 1930 a new large modern cinema, The Regal, was built between the other two cinemas. It boasted a car-park at the rear.

On the opening night crowds gathered outside the doors to see the arrival of Jack Hulbert and his wife Cicely Courtneige, who were the stars of the film to be shown that evening - Jack's The Boy.

What a wonderful place that building was to a ten-year-old girl!

The front few rows of seats cost 6d, so I could get in for three pennies on a Saturday afternoon - the next rows cost 9d, and the back seats were 1s.

We would be enthralled for hours. First the dark red velvet curtains swung back to reveal delicate ruched curtains which, in turn, revealed the big screen as the lights were dimmed.

I saw Jack's The Boy, then a film called Delicious starring Janet Gaynor, and later Jack Buchanan in Goodnight Vienna.

Ladies sitting in the back seats could order tea to be served to them at 4pm by a waitress from the restaurant upstairs.

The balcony seats always fascinated me, but I had to wait for a few years, until a boyfriend took me to the cinema, and we sat up there.

Nora Hough

A PICTURE PALACE AT THE SEASIDE - THE RIVIERA CINEMA AT TEIGNMOUTH PHOTOGRAPHED BY
GEORGE LORIMER IN 1985

OLNEY'S BEST

MY PICTURE-going days go back to the Jazz Age of the early 1920s, the era of the silent film.

The local cinema in the small market town of Olney in North Bucks was a converted hall built originally for social events, concerts etc. It had a level central aisle with rows of hard wooden seats on either side and an elevated stage.

Electricity had not yet reached the town, but a petrol-driven generator overcame this difficulty.

The outside entrance was flanked by two windows. These were blacked out and a cabin was erected to house the sole projector whose lens protruded through one of the windows.

The owner was the projectionist who painstakingly hand-cranked the machine. With only the one projector, the patrons were obliged to sit in the dark while the reels were changed.

Just as the action reached a critical point, the reels would come to an end.

As reels lasted ten minutes and nine reels were involved, tension and anticipation were put to the test.

The films were accompanied by a lady pianist. Programmes changed mid week so on a Monday or Thursday evening the musical accompaniment tended to be unrehearsed and a trifle erratic.

Improvements were made when the ownership changed hands. A projection room containing two projectors was erected above the central entrance.

The highspot of the silent film era for the cinema was the showing of Ramon Novarro in the 1926 version of Ben Hur. In the galley slave scenes, the shackled slaves rowed to the beat of a drum and the rattling of chains behind the screen!

With yet another change in ownership the generator was shut down and mains electricity installed. The 'live orchestra' - piano and violin - was replaced by two gramophone turntables billed as 'The Hidden Orchestra', ensuring a continuous musical accompaniment.

Who could forget the silent film of Edith Cavell? In the scene where she was praying in her cell before her execution, the cinema management played a record of Dame Clara Butt singing Abide With Me. It was an emotional moment.

In the summer of 1930 the Olney cinema was converted to sound. After a week's closure we were introduced to this new medium with Charles Farrell and Janet Gaynor in Sunnyside Up.

As I was just entering my teens, an impressionable age, I sat enthralled as Janet sang If I Had a Talking Picture of You.

In 1935 Sidney Bernstein had the air-conditioned super cinema, the Granada, built at Bedford - a truly luxurious cinema complete with organ. I transferred my allegiance from the Olney cinema to the Granada. It finally closed in the 1960s.

A F Johnson

ABOVE: THE ROYALTY CINEMA IN DARTMOUTH PHOTOGRAPHED BY GEORGE LORIMER IN 1985

A MESS IN ITALY

IN 1942 while in Naples with the Eighth Army, a group of us were invited by American GIs to a film show in their canteen - a new movie from 'back home'.

We sat in chairs facing a rather flimsy portable screen with an audience becoming impatient as the two soldiers operating the 16mm projector were having trouble with the light source of the machine.

Things got going at last, to cheers from the khaki-clad audience.

The film was Errol Flynn in Gentleman Jim. He played Corbett the boxer fighting John L Sullivan for the championship in 1892 in New Orleans.

As we watched the fight on the quivering screen, disaster struck as the projector suddenly burst into flames. The audience yelled loudly as a hefty American sergeant quelled the flames with a fire extinguisher.

Unknown to me at the time, Audie Murphy was in the audience - the man who would become the most highly decorated GI of the war.

George Greengrass

Your favourite pin-ups

★ *Stewart Granger* ★

(1913 - 1993)

With rapier poised for an exciting fight, the romantic-looking Stewart Granger was a familiar figure on cinema screens in the 1940s and 50s. Perhaps pictures of him graced your bedroom wall as a teenager!

In 'Scaramouche' (1952) he was involved in the longest sword fight ever filmed - around seven minutes - with Mel Ferrer.

In a series of adventure films in the 1950s he appeared with many of the glamorous leading ladies of the time such as Deborah Kerr in 'King Solomon's Mines' and 'The Prisoner of Zenda', Elizabeth Taylor in 'Beau Brummell' and Ava Gardner in 'Bhowani Junction'.

Off-screen antics

SO EMBARRASSING

WHEN I was young, during the war, we didn't have any spare cash to go to the cinema. However a neighbour, Mrs Beedham, would come round each Saturday afternoon. She would rattle her long walking stick on our railings and call down to me to see if I would like to go to the pictures with her.

Her stick was like the sort that Queen Mary once used, with a silver knob on the end.

Let me put you in the picture. I was at that awkward age where you think that everyone is looking at you.

I was quite small for my age, whereas Mrs Beedham was exceedingly fat. She had a heart of gold and meant well, but I would be embarrassed walking alongside her as she swayed from side to side as we went to catch the bus.

She always sat on the seats just inside the door that face each other, she couldn't fit into the others, and in a voice that would have been excellent in a theatre, spoke to everyone who passed.

Arriving at the theatre for the matinee, we had to go to the side entrance in the Capitol Cinema. There, at the very front of the stalls, the seats did not have any arms. She would buy three tickets - one for me and two for her.

Being the matinee, these seats would be full of children ready to cheer their hero and boo at the villain.

I sat like a little mouse, trying to be as inconspicuous as possible and hoping that none of my friends would see me. I tried to make out that Mrs Beedham wasn't with me.

When the lights went out I began to enjoy myself - but not for long. As the other children's voices became louder, Mrs Beedham got more and more angry as she could not follow the film.

Up would come her stick and she would poke any children who were not behaving.

When the interval came and the lights were turned on, the miscreants would turn to get a good view of who had been poking them. And I would start to cringe again.

I'm sure that her voice could be heard in the circle. Usually the manager came to see what was happening, and tried to calm everyone down before the lights went out for the second half.

I did appreciate her taking me and sharing her sweet ration with me, but I found it very hard to enjoy the films.

My mother said I would have to tell her myself I didn't want to go. But I never had the courage to do so.

Looking back I can see the funny side of it.

Margaret E Griffiths

BLACK MARKET BANANAS

AS A very young library assistant in Glasgow in the late 1930s, I was very impressed by the impact made on readers by the Margaret Mitchell novel Gone With the Wind. So impressed that on one of my first leaves home from the WAAF I was delighted to find that this was to be brought to life and shown in a city cinema.

My sister and I went along, interested to find how Vivien Leigh and Clark Gable had interpreted the roles of Scarlett and Rhett.

While we queued to get in we were entertained by many buskers, and, on this occasion, with the unexpected sale of bananas!

A small shabby van drew up, two men emerged and quickly sold their fruit before jumping into the van again and making off at speed.

Black market of course. But who could resist such a treat - we did enjoy them as we watched this truly wonderful story on film.

Jeannie Peck

FREE HAIR CREAM

IN THE 1930s when I was 13 I went to the Granada cinema in Tooting, London, to see Warner Oland in Charlie Chan at the Circus.

I went to the toilet. I saw a glass bowl over the sink while I was washing my hands. I thought - 'Oh, free green hair cream' (I'd never heard of liquid soap).

It made my head feel tight and solid. I was glad it wasn't raining when I came out.

John Cole

LONG IN THE TOOTH

THE GRANADA in Tooting was truly like a palace. I went there from 1920 to 1990.

They used to charge 5p for pensioners in the afternoons and a friend and I went regularly.

She used to love Carry On films and once she laughed so much her false teeth dropped out. We had to get the usherette to help us find them.

Luckily they were intact.

Daisy Heather

IT WAS DIFFERENT THEN

MY HUSBAND says he can remember as a child going to the Saturday matinee pictures for the price of a clean, empty jam jar. If he took one in he had to share a seat, but if he were fortunate and his mother gave him two, he could have his own seat.

I remember, as a child, biking to the next village with my two cousins to see a black and white private detective film.

The cinema backed onto the railway track so everyone hung onto their seats when the steam trains went past. The screen vibrated as well.

I liked it best going to the cinema with my eldest sister who in those days was an usherette. She used to buy me a selection of sweets to keep me quiet and so I wouldn't tell our mum she was sitting in the back row with her boyfriend.

Rosemary Medland

ABOVE: BEST FRIENDS JUNE AND MYRA AS LITTLE GIRLS IN A FAMILY PHOTOGRAPH TAKEN IN 1937

MORTIFIED BY A MESSAGE

IN THE town of Irvine, Ayrshire there were four picture houses - Greens, the Regal, Palace and the Kyle. During the 1930s they were the hive of entertainment.

The Kyle was the poshest with muted lighting, curtains which changed colour, crushed velvet seats and soft music. On Saturdays, when seats could be reserved, the manager, resplendent in evening suit, stood in the foyer to greet the customers, smiling and nodding as they filed in.

My best friend, June Anderson and myself, went to the Kyle one Saturday. We enjoyed the films so much that we sat round for a second time to see them all again!

Suddenly we were astonished when, after the adverts, a sign flashed up on the screen saying 'Will Myra Rubie - me - and June Anderson return home at once'.

There outside stood our mothers wielding their umbrellas to whack us home for being out late without permission.

We girls were mortified over the announcement up there on the flickering screen for all to see.

Myra Shreeve

BODIES LINED UP IN THE FOYER

THE FILM I remember most of all was Birth of a Baby, although I only ever saw the beginning.

I was a member of the St John's Ambulance Brigade, Mitcham Division. I was on duty at the Granada in Tooting.

All was fairly normal until the poor woman started to give birth. As soon as the head of the baby appeared people started to pass out all over the cinema. We had to get them out into the foyer which soon began to look like a battle field with bodies lined up in neat array.

We all worked hard that night and, fortunately, none of the 'patients' suffered ill effects afterwards.

Ron Sillence

GOING WITH UNCLE EDWARD

DURING AND just after the war my Uncle Edward would take me with him to his beloved flicks.

For some reason he liked to go to the nearest ones in summer and the furthest ones in winter. He'd trail me in my thin, worn-out shoes through the snow to the Commodore, which was miles away.

He'd march straight on with me in tow and never looked back to see where I was. Eventually he'd sit on a step and take a breather while I would catch up.

He never quite got the names of the stars right. Humphrey Bogart he called Jumpty Bog and Barbara Stanwyck he re-christened Barbara Sandwich. But I'm sure they wouldn't have minded - he paid often enough to see them.

Children loved him. In those days the old 'A' certificate meant that children could only be admitted if accompanied by an adult. Often they'd be a gang hanging around outside until Uncle Edward came along to save the day.

They'd give him their money and "One and nine halves," Uncle Edward would say to the cashier. I'm sure they were all wise to the little ruse.

In we would all troop and to make it look more authentic, they would all sit near us.

There my Uncle Edward would sit, surrounded by children, puffing vigorously on his pipe and enveloping us all in a cloud of smoke.

He liked to get there early so he could get a good seat. When he took me to the Apollo, we were the first to arrive.

We stood at the back surveying the auditorium and were deciding where to sit when I said I needed to go to the toilet. Uncle Edward was adamant we got to our seats first and insisted I sit down with him in the middle of the empty auditorium. Only then did he say it was safe for us to go to the toilet.

When we got back, there were now just two people sitting in the cinema, in the very seats that we had vacated. "Blast!" said Uncle Edward, "someone's taken our seats!"

Years later when I was working I returned Uncle Edward's kindness by taking him to the flicks to treat him.

Times had changed and there was a nude scene in one of the films. In the dark, silent auditorium Uncle Edward shouted out, "God! They've got no clothes on!".

A short while later, when he'd had the chance to reflect and reassure himself, he informed the audience, "They've got clothes on really, but you can't see 'em".

Richard Moore

Too Tight

THE CINEMA was packed to see Greta Garbo as the Polish countess in Countess Walewska, pleading to Napoleon (Charles Boyer) not to invade her country.

The silence was pregnant with anticipation of the love scene. Suddenly, from a little boy, came a piercing whisper, "Mum, his trousers are too tight!".

Elva Bannerman

Go On, Errol!

DURING THE war my mother took my grandmother and myself, aged about nine, to the local cinema.

We went to see a war film featuring Errol Flynn as a pilot. During the most tense and exciting air battle my grandmother stood up and shouted, "Get your speed up Errol, he's behind you!"

Hazel M deLuce

Vest in the Dark

MY MOTHER was disgusted to learn that my husband and I were going to have a baby, and I had expected her to be so thrilled. Her friend was equally censorious that we should reproduce in wartime.

They forced me to go with them to see Gone With the Wind. I was disgruntled because I'd read the book and didn't like it.

To show my displeasure I took my knitting and knitted a whole baby's vest during the showing.

Dolly Harmer

Alice Did the Trick

I SAW MY first film in 1948. I was fourteen and had just come out of hospital after seven years of a disabling illness.

My parents decided to take me to the Kinema, our local flea pit, and I was very excited.

They had to push me in my wheelchair to Plumstead from Abbeywood, quite a distance. Then I had to be transferred to a seat, fire regulations not allowing a disabled person to stay in a wheelchair blocking the aisle.

Badgers Green came on first - a slow saga of the village green and cricket. There must have been a story, but I don't remember, it was so boring.

The big film was Eureka Stockade starring Chips Rafferty. By today's standards it would be slow, but then it was classed as violent as it was set in Australia during the gold rush.

I know that I was so disappointed in what was to have been a big treat.

Later my parents tried again with Fire Down Below starring Rita Hayworth, but it still wasn't suitable for a fourteen year old.

Walt Disney's Alice in Wonderland changed it all - from then on the cinema was magic.

Cathy Byatt

No Time for a Picnic

IN THE 1930s my mother, grandma and I went to an afternoon matinee at the Palace Cinema in Tottenham, London.

Grandma liked to sit in the circle, so we walked up the staircase past photographs of glamorous stars lining the walls.

We always arrived early when there were plenty of empty seats. Just as well, for like Goldilocks, Grandma would have to try several until she found one that was just right!

The organist played popular music until the programme was due to start. Then maestro and instrument descended into the nether regions of the cinema. Lights dimmed and in the expectant hush Grandma produced a paper bag of boiled sweets or toffees, whose wrapping cracked noisily when removed.

Later, and usually when dimpled Shirley Temple was beguiling some crotchety adult, or Errol Flynn engaged in a sword fight with a foe, the rustling of paper began again.

This time a packet of fish-paste sandwiches - salmon and shrimp, or bloater - was passed along. Then came oranges. In the darkness the tangy scent drifted around the circle audience.

One day, watching Errol as Robin Hood clad in a fetching outfit of Lincoln green, my mother lost her temper with Grandma.

"I thought we'd come to see a film, not to have a picnic!"

Secretly, I think she fancied Errol Flynn and hated to be distracted from his debonair charms!

Joan Coates

SHAME ON MY SHOES

I WENT TO the Blue Hall in Edgware Road with my first date, and left in shame.

The heating pipes ran under the row of seats in front. I put my feet on them and when we got up to go, the soles of my shoes had melted!

Peggy Cuckoo

GRANDMA'S DELIGHT

MY GRANDMA loved going to the pictures. She would always insist on sitting in the last seat of a middle row. When people needed to get past her to their seats, she would tut tut loudly and get up slowly with much fuss.

She liked to make loud comments, too, and I was at times forced to say sshh. She also loved having a choc ice. When she'd finished it she would settle down again and nod off to sleep.

I frequently needed to nudge her if she snored, and woe betide anyone who needed to get past her.

Shirley Page

THE NEXT MARY PICKFORD

A CINEMA OPENED at the Elephant and Castle in London when I was in my early teens.

One Sunday we could have a screen test. We filed past cameramen, there was a flash, and we were done.

The results would be shown the following week - all of us went home with visions of Hollywood to keep us going. Well, Mary Pickford had just been discovered and I knew I was star material.

When I saw the result on the screen the following week I hid my head in shame.

I looked awful, but it gave the audience a good laugh.

Molly Nixon

I BELIEVE THAT the film Rio Rita, which my mother saw in the early 1930s, started it all!

As a child in the Second World War, mum and I were avid film fans. We lived in North London and on Saturdays, once we had done our weekend shopping, we would usually visit the cinema - sometimes twice.

I have many memories of this period in our lives, which because of the war was not exactly the happiest of times. Nevertheless, mum and I used to make the most of things and laugh in adversity.

Rationing meant that we took what we could get to eat to the pictures. One day we had a rare box of dates, most of which we ate in the darkness. Imagine our horror when the lights went up and the box was crawling with maggots!

Another time, we emerged from the State Cinema in Kilburn to find that all transport had come to a standstill due to a pea-souper fog which had come down.

Mum and I had to walk all the way home to Cricklewood. There were no lights because of the blackout and we literally couldn't see a hand in front of our face, so many times we found ourselves in people's front gardens, bumping into hedges, falling over steps.

When we finally arrived home we looked like a couple of pandas with black rings around our eyes from the smog.

Rita Tobin

IN 1946 I was a junior shorthand typist, aged 16 and on a weekly wage of 42s.

A cadet from a nearby officer cadet training unit invited me to the cinema. Ever frugal, I was quite happy to opt for the 1s 9d's. He obviously didn't want to sit with the common herd, so it had to be the 2s 6d's upstairs.

When it was time to pay, he looked all sheepish and said his cheque - from wherever - hadn't arrived. So, to save face, I paid for us both. This meant I had to 'rob Peter to pay Paul' all the next week.

I can laugh about it now but it wasn't funny at the time.

So if you recognise yourself, Hugh from Scotland, you owe me five bob plus interest!

Margaret Browne

DURING THE 1930s we always spent Saturday afternoons at the pictures. My mother always came with us, and often she would escort about 20 other kids if the film was an 'A' certificate.

Our cinema was the Regal at St Ives, near Huntingdon. It was close to the river, and on a few occasions flood water got into the building.

When I was away in the ATS, Mum sent me a letter saying that she had just been to the flooded cinema, and the film they showed was Mutiny on the Bounty.

Vera Mitchell

LISTENING TO THE MUSIC

WHEN I was a little girl we lived next to a picture house - that's what they were called in my day - where they showed silent films.

My bedroom wall was next to it and when I lay in bed I could tell what kind of picture was showing by the music which a lady played on the piano. It was very quick and noisy for westerns and nice and quiet for love stories.

D Harris

SHORT PUFFS

MY FRIEND Valerie lived next door and we used to go to the pictures three or four times a week.

Before going we went to a little sweet shop on the corner to buy five Weights. We would come home, cut them in half to make them go further, and take a hair grip to hold them, because they were so small. About three puffs and they were gone.

Iris Doe

THE BEST NEWS EVER

DURING THE war, my mother used to go to the flicks for a good cry. You can imagine her shock when the news came on and they showed prisoners of war in Germany being released - and there was my dad right at the front.

She screamed out and leapt up and laddered her precious nylons. They had been given to her by an American serviceman, who used to frequent the shop in which she worked, in thanks for her polite and kind manner when serving him.

After the performance had finished, the theatre manager allowed my mother to sit in the front row of the empty cinema while he ran the news again. When it got to the bit with my dad in it, he stopped the film for a few moments and my mother went right up, as close as she could, and was crying her eyes out in excitement.

My father was amazed when he got home to find that mum had got everything ready for him.

"How on earth did you know?" he asked in bewilderment.

"A little bird told me!" she said, referring to the rooster who 'introduced' the news.

Rita Wigginton

HALFPENNY SHORT

MY BOYFRIEND (now my husband) was home on leave from the Navy in 1944.

He took me to the local cinema. He put his money down for the cashier, asked for two 1s 9d seats and said, "And I owe you a halfpenny".

Was my face red! But we got our seats - it must have been the uniform!

June Johnson

I'VE BEEN SHOT!

I STARTED GOING to the cinema when I was very small. My parents always took a bottle of pop for me to drink as I never failed to get thirsty.

One night we were engrossed in a western with lots of shooting.

There was a loud bang and dad suddenly clutched his chest. "My God, Min," he gasped to my mother, "I've been shot".

What he'd thought was blood on his shirt was the pop which had poured out of the bottle when it exploded due to a build up of gases!

We had to walk back from the cinema in Uphall along the disused railway from Pumpherston, about two miles.

When I grumbled about my legs being tired dad would say, "Look up at the stars. By the time you've counted them all you'll be home".

Chrissy Gibbs

COVER YOUR HEAD

WE'D BEEN studying the Elizabethans at school and it was suggested we ask our parents to take us to see a film about Sir Francis Drake.

Mum was not very keen, however she took me, and thought it all very boring. I don't remember much at all, not even the title because I began to feel quite ill and just longed for the film to finish so we could go home.

When we came out of the darkness into the large, well-lit foyer, mum looked at me and said, "Cover your head with my scarf and keep your head down". I wondered why, then she muttered, "I can't afford a taxi, we'll have to catch a bus. Keep your head down."

It was a two-mile journey and we had to stand on the crowded bus. When we arrived home I looked in the mirror - I was covered in a livid red rash.

I never discovered how many pupils in my class saw the film as I was off sick for a couple of weeks with a severe dose of German Measles.

Also I never knew how many people I infected in the cinema, or on the journey home!

Mavis Barrick

NOTHING TO DO WITH US

WHEN MY wife was working late in her office, we'd arrange to meet outside the cinema.

Between her office and the cinema she had to cross the cobbled courtyard of a garage. One night when it was dark, she didn't notice that the cobbles were covered in oil and petrol. She slid and fell down.

Fortunately she was only shaken, but her coat was covered in oil and petrol and gave off a real garage aroma. She carried on to meet me and we went in to the cinema. She took off her coat, put in on the floor and we took our seats.

The cinema was very warm and her coat began to give off a really strong smell. Several couples nearby got up and went and sat elsewhere. No one came to sit near us all evening.

We sat in splendid isolation, like two victims of the plague, and tried to pretend that the smell had nothing whatever to do with us.

Ron Sheppeard

TUG OF WAR IN THE BALCONY

MY FRIEND Shirley and I were both fifteen during the war and were crazy about Errol Flynn.

When his latest film came to one of the cinemas in Southport, wild horses wouldn't have kept us away.

We were supposed to be playing tennis on the school courts but we leapt onto our bicycles and raced into town.

We parked our bikes outside the cinema and locked them and, because you couldn't get bicycle pumps during the war, I took mine into the cinema with me.

We were a bit late and the film had started. The cinema was very full and very dark. An usherette came with her torch and, seizing hold of the end of my bicycle pump, she led us right down to the front row of the balcony and we had two of the best seats in the house.

We sat down and then the tug of war began with my bicycle pump. The usherette tugged fiercely and I hung on tightly. After a couple of minutes I said, "Why do you want my bicycle pump?".

"Oh no," she said, engulfed with embarrassment, "I thought it was your deaf apparatus and I wanted to plug it in".

She fled and we spent the next twenty minutes trying to stop giggling.

Joyce Thomson

INTENDING TO IMPRESS

AS A teenager I was taken on a first date to the Trocadero at the Elephant and Castle in London. It was one of the first picture 'palaces' and the interior had to be seen to be believed. There were twinkling stars shining down on an Eastern setting - quite out of this world.

The young man, no doubt intending to impress, had bought tickets for the most expensive seats, 2s 6d each.

As we made our way up to the first row of the circle, going backwards chatting to me, he unconsciously followed the two women ahead of him straight into the ladies. The door closed behind him with an ominous click.

Seconds later he emerged shocked and scarlet of face, his air of assurance completely gone. I'm afraid his evening had been entirely spoiled at the outset - in those days such a happening was the height of embarrassment.

The few times I met him afterwards we went for bus rides.

Madeleine Jennings

FEAR OF DRACULA

WHEN I was fourteen my friend and I walked into town to see the new Dracula film starring Christopher Lee. The film terrified us and we sat holding hands in fear all night.

On the way home the road was narrow and dark. The wind howled and waved the branches of the trees growing on each side. There was a full moon, no street lights - and no one about to save us.

Sheer terror made us pick up our heels and run. We didn't stop till we reached home!

A Price

✫ *Doris Day* ✫

(BORN 1924)

FOR MANY A YOUNG MAN IN THE FIFTIES
SHE WAS THE PERFECT GIRL NEXT DOOR!
THE ROLES SHE PLAYED MADE HER
EQUALLY LIKED BY BOTH MEN AND
WOMEN AND IN THE 1950s DORIS DAY
LOOKALIKES WERE EVERYWHERE
(PERHAPS YOU WERE ONE).
SHE BEGAN HER CAREER AS A SINGER
WITH BIG BANDS AND BECAME A
POPULAR RADIO STAR.
'CALAMITY JANE' WITH HOWARD KEEL
WAS HER FIRST BIG SUCCESS.
OTHER MUSICAL FILMS LIKE 'YOUNG AT
HEART', WITH FRANK SINATRA,
'LOVE ME OR LEAVE ME' AND
'PAJAMA GAME' FOLLOWED.
A SERIES OF LIGHT ROMANTIC COMEDIES
WITH CO-STAR ROCK HUDSON KEPT FANS
HAPPY AND SHE REMAINED A TOP BOX-
OFFICE STAR WELL IN THE 1960s. SHE
RETIRED FROM FILMS IN 1968.

Star struck

WE STUCK THEIR PHOTOGRAPHS ON OUR WALLS,
COPIED THEIR CLOTHES AND HAIRSTYLES - WE WERE
INFATUATED BY THESE LARGER-THAN-LIFE
GLAMOROUS PEOPLE UP THERE ON THE SCREEN...

TOO SHY

MY ALL-TIME favourite was Betty Grable. Her films were full of colour, songs and the good guys always won the day.

I remember sitting through a continuous performance while my dad waited outside wondering where I was at 9pm.

My other favourite was Richard Attenborough and when he was in Brighton filming Brighton Rock he passed me coming out of a cafe in Queens Road. My knees went weak, but I was too shy to ask for an autograph.

Mary Poulton

TRANSPORTED BY THE WICKED LADY

SHIRLEY TEMPLE films were the ones that I enjoyed most as a small child and I think I was probably taken to see most of them. How I envied Shirley, especially those bouncing corkscrew curls - my hair was dark and shingled, not a corkscrew in sight.

It makes me cringe now to think that I also liked the songs and would try to sing Animal Crackers in My Soup. How my poor mother must have suffered! One Christmas I was given a Shirley Temple book and this was my favourite reading material for a long time.

Snow White and the Seven Dwarfs was around at this time but the overall enjoyment was spoiled for me by the terrifying appearance of the wicked witch, although I'm not sure that mum knew quite how much it frightened me.

As I had a Wednesday half-holiday from school, mum and I had a regular date for a matinee performance.

No doubt we saw many American films, but, even more than fifty years later, it is British-made films that stay in my mind, particularly those featuring Stewart Granger (my hero!), James Mason, Margaret Lockwood (complete with beauty spot; was it there in her very early films?), Phyllis Calvert and Patricia Roc.

How I was transported at the antics of The Wicked Lady, and sighed at the romantic Frenchman's Creek, which also introduced me to Debussy's Clair du Lune.

Perhaps Stewart Granger did have a lasting effect on me, for the man that I finally married could, perhaps, be said to have had a passing resemblance to him!

Bernice Russell

MYSTERY WITH ANNA MAY WONG

I WENT TO my first picture show at the Roxy, Burton-on-Trent. I sat between our two servants Maude and Ivy - yes, we actually had servants - and my mother allowed them to take me to the pictures.

By my side sat Ivy and I was well aware of her pretty presence.

We watched heart-throb Mary Pickford in a film called Suds. She was a little laundress who washed the shirts of a dashing young man, and her limpid eyes gazed upon him. And they fell in love and fortune smiled upon them.

But that young man was not only on the silver screen. He was sitting in the sixpenny seats too - me! Such was the magic of the movies.

Years later I was sent to a boarding school in Rhyl, North Wales where we were fenced in from the outside world. No movies, no girls. But a mile down the road was a picture palace.

One day I crawled through the hedge and broke bounds, and with my sixpenny pocket money, slipped into the forbidden darkness where I watched, fascinated, the story of Alf's Button played by Leslie Henson. Rub the button and a genie appeared to do Alf's bidding.

But, better still, the second picture was a tale of murder and mystery with Anna May Wong, a voluptuous dancer in a night club.

What a story of whispered naughtiness did I relate to my envious school friends!

But next day in the headmaster's study it was "Hold out your hand" and I felt the crack, crack, crack of that bendy cane he kept for such occasions.

But it was worth it. Oh, very much so.

How the pictures influenced us. Do you remember Matheson Lang in The Scarlet Pimpernel? As a teenager, for weeks I'd dress up in my dressing gown and strut around with my brother, who preferred to work the guillotine.

It was a dream world of our own.

Arthur Fielder

A GOOD LAUGH

THERE WERE enormous queues when my mother took me to see Charlie Chaplin and Jackie Coogan in The Kid.

We discussed each Chaplin picture for days afterwards. Who can ever forget the scene where he eats his boots, laces and all, in The Gold Rush.

Another marvellous comic was Buster Keaton with the frozen face. I loved the episode where he stands in the front of a house which collapses around him, leaving him miraculously unscathed.

Each week's visit to the cinema we laughed at the crazy antics of the Keystone Cops in their ancient Model T Ford, boss-eyed Ben Turpin, Charlie Chase, Chester Conklin, Larry Lemur and many others.

We collected glossy photos from film magazines of our favourites: swashbuckling Douglas Fairbanks, the Western idols such as Tom Mix, Buck Jones and strong, silent William S Hart.

Arthur Clarke

I loved dear Spencer Tracy,
Tyrone and Errol Flynn,
Tom Brown and Richard Cromwell,
Andy Hardy's grin.
They set my heart a'thumping,
emotions in a whirl.
But that was all so long ago
when I was but a girl.

How I longed to be like Colbert
or maybe Betty Grable,
To be kissed and pressed against the
chest of handsome Mr Gable.
On one or two occasions
each and every week
For the price of sixpence,
romantic thrills I'd seek.

Lugosi, Lorre, Boris,
they scared me half to death!
While the daring feats of Fairbanks
fairly took my breath.
The voices of Nelson Eddy
and John Boles made me swoon
And so did Tony, Martin - and Bing,
the King of Croon.

Beery, Mari Dressler and
Jolson's Singing Fool,
Charming Valentino and
Will Hay's crazy school,
Our Gang and Shirley Temple;
how she could sing and dance,
With Rin-Tin-Tin the wonder dog,
the villain had no chance.

The programme was quite lengthy
with pictures A and B,
Pathe News or Movietone,
the March of Time to see.
We didn't have an interval
for organs were the rage,
And sometimes for an extra treat
we saw an act on stage.

Now the picture palaces
are rarely to be seen,
Old or dead those idols
of the silver screen.
Should you feel nostalgic
for this era of the past,
Then, my friend, just like for me,
the sand is running fast.

Madeleine J Croll

JEANNE CRAIN WAS MY IDEAL

WHEN I was in my teens and living on the Isle of Wight I worked part-time at the local cinema.

My favourite film of all time was State Fair with Dick Haymes and Jeanne Crain.

She was my ideal and I copied her dark brown wavy hair flowing over the shoulders, floating summer dress with a stiff-layered net waist-slip and joy - oh joy! - I managed to buy a pair of white strappy sandals almost identical to the ones she wore in the film.

My mother was horrified and said the heels were too high, which they were. But I didn't care, for after a few tottering steps and getting the balance right, I was away.

Heather Peddar

A SURPRISE IN THE INTERVAL

I ALMOST LIVED at the cinema when I was a teenager in the 1950s. I was a great fan of Margaret Lockwood after seeing The Wicked Lady, so imagine how thrilled I was when she appeared in our local cinema.

I can still hear the gasps from the cinema audience as she walked on the stage during the interval. There hadn't been much advance publicity.

For about ten minutes she talked about her latest film Laughing Ann.

I had never seen a real film star in the flesh, only on the screen. I wrote to her just before she died and she sent me a lovely letter and signed photo which I treasure.

John Miles

STARS IN THE GARDEN

ARE THERE any other film fans who remember the Film Star Garden Party held at Morden Hall Park on June 18, 1949?

Just getting there from Southampton was quite an adventure for my friend Rosie and I when we were both seventeen.

Proudly clutching my very first camera, I pushed through the crowds trying to snap the stars.

Sadly, when the film was developed, most of the film stars were obscured by

people standing in the way. I just have these two pictures to remind me of that memorable day.

One of the actors I was vainly chasing on that sunny afternoon was Hubert Gregg. Unfortunately in those days he was a very fast mover, so I didn't succeed in getting him on film.

My friend Rose was besotted by Gary Cooper, but David Niven and Michael Wilding were my ideal men. Oh, and if only I could have looked like Margaret Lockwood!

Jean Saffin

ABOVE: ANNE CRAWFORD WITH GRIFFITH JONES AND SALLY GRAY IN THE BACKGROUND

LEFT: RICHARD ATTENBOROUGH

66

MY DAY OF FAME

SOMETIMES, IN the late 1940s and early 50s, I would go to the pictures three times a week. I would queue for hours to see the stars I idolised.

Musicals were a favourite and I'd sit watching the likes of Jane Powell, Gene Kelly and Cyd Charisse and be transported into another world, a world full of beautiful people, wearing gorgeous clothes, dancing across the screen with such grace.

Around 1949, I saw a British film set in Blackpool called Forbidden starring Hazel Court. Afterwards, when I came out of the cinema, I noticed they were running a competition about the film, so I entered it.

I was amazed to win. My prize was a holiday for two at a Butlins holiday camp but, best of all, I was to be presented with my prize by Hazel Court on the stage of a big London cinema.

I was incredibly nervous before meeting Miss Court and then somewhat disillusioned because she was covered in freckles - they didn't show on the screen.

She also seemed a little aloof but I guess she was bored by yet another personal appearance. But I was very thrilled, especially when the photographers took my photo standing alongside Miss Court.

Although I was promised copies of these pictures, I never did receive them. I was a very disappointed fifteen-year-old as I'd been so looking forward to showing my friends my day of fame.

I'm now 63 but can't say I have ever got over my star-struck days. Musicals and black and white films feature widely in my video collection.

Jean Moore

DRESSING LIKE SHIRLEY

MY MOTHER was rather clever with a needle and whenever a Shirley Temple film was on we had to go, me being the same age as Shirley.

During the film my mother made a mental note of what Shirley was wearing. As soon as we got home out came the sheets of paper and my mother made me stand on the table while she cut and pinned the paper onto me.

As time passed by and we had to have dress coupons, more often than not my dress was made out of one of my mother's. Not quite like Shirley's!

Mary Hebron

YOU AIN'T HEARD NOTHING YET!

IN 1927 when I was four we lived in East London. One day my mother came home full of excitement, saying she had seen a large bill-board outside our local cinema announcing that the first talking picture would arrive there in a few weeks time.

Mother was determined to go and see it. Dad wasn't too keen on the idea, though he did enjoy the old silent films. He remarked that this new-fangled stuff wouldn't last long, also that the stars' voices would never be heard over the piano playing in the pit!

All the talk in the town was about this wonderful American film - The Jazz Singer - starring Al Jolson, the well-known American singer and actor.

I was so anxious to go, and kept on to mother about it, especially as I had told all my playmates I would see it, although I don't think they believed me!

Eventually I had my way.

We both arrived outside the cinema and found the queue of people nearly round the block, everyone chatting about this marvellous invention.

We waited nearly an hour before we managed to get inside.

An expectant hush filled the cinema, when after a few silent reels of the film and silent acting, Al Jolson was seen seated at a piano with his mother standing beside him listening… a sound of piano notes were heard and, to our delight, Jolson then spoke quite clearly… "Listen to this Ma - 'cos you ain't heard nothing yet!"

He continued to play, while we were left gasping and clapping, everyone wanting more of this wonderful experience.

My mother had tears in her eyes, and said, "Well dear, today you've heard and seen something you'll never forget".

Nancy Lowther

DAYS OF POPCORN AND PECK

How well I remember those days long ago,
When life was so simple, romantic and slow.
We'd queue for the flicks in such orderly lines,
Then settle ourselves in the front 'one and nines'.
The old crowing cockerel would herald the news,
But Mickey and Minnie soon banished the blues.
And what did we care for a crick in the neck
With a large bag of popcorn, and Gregory Peck?

And oh, to recapture the glorious thrill
Of Granger the Dashing who fenced with such skill,
Who tackled a dozen wild swordsmen - or more -
And soon had their corpses lined up on the floor.
The hand of the lady he'd readily claim,
Miss Margaret Lockwood (of beauty-spot fame).
And as they embraced in the star-spangled night
Our souls were transported to realms of delight.

Now at the pictures, I weep with despair,
The hero has nose-rings and wild orange hair!
He can't fight a duel, for he hasn't the guts,
And he clobbers his woman and tells her she's nuts!
I can't say I blame him, she's hardly a saint,
She cusses and bawls - and a lady, she ain't!
Oh give me the days of popcorn and Peck
In the front 'one and nines' with a crick in me neck!

Gwen Downey

THE MAGIC OF CARMEN

MY MOTHER, being a devoted film fan, took us to the cinema every week and there were the wonderful Saturday morning outings too.

I grew up with all those wonderful stars of the 40s - the beautiful women, who looked like women and the handsome male heroes.

I never wanted to come out of the cinema.

I loved the glamour of Dorothy Lamour, Veronica Lake, Ann Sheridan, Betty Grable - I could go on forever…

But the all-time favourite that I idolised was Carmen Miranda. I've built up a collection of memorabilia on her over the years and I have a wonderful tribute room to her memory.

I have had various TV companies here when doing specials on Carmen or South America to photograph my collection and I even went as far as to name one of my daughters Carmen Miranda and have her name tattooed on my arm! How's that for devotion!

Carmen gave me a lot of pleasure over the years and still does by viewing her video films or playing her records and even today, more than 40 years after her death, she is still remembered by many.

I still go to the cinema but the old magic is gone. We had the best era and I think myself lucky to have been able to enjoy it all.

Ivan Jack

DRESSING LIKE GANGSTERS

I REMEMBER WELL the pre-war golden days of the cinema. We would cheerfully queue for upwards of two hours in all weathers to see our celluloid heroes.

My brother and I would go first to our local Woolworths to chat up a pair of pretty girls - all the attractive girls seemed to work in Woolies.

We would ape the dress of the stars, especially the gangster stars like James Cagney, George Raft, Bogart and others. We would wear long blue Melton overcoats, trilby hats and white silk scarves.

The girls would do their part by trying to look like gangsters' molls, as they were termed. They'd wear a knee-length tight black skirt, sometimes with a split at the side, black silk stockings with seams and a small Robin Hood hat to complete a picture of utter loveliness.

Their lipstick would be bright red, and no girl would be seen without her powder compact. To have a shiny nose was the ultimate disgrace.

Before venturing out, of course we would all receive strict orders from our dear parents to be in by 11 o'clock or else…

We would watch cartoons, a B picture, a live stage show with someone like Billy Cotton, a big band, Mantovani, or other shows of that period, as well as the news and the big film. We would often be in the cinema for five hours or more.

What value for 1s 9d!

Richard Carter

THE WOMEN SHRIEKED WITH DELIGHT

IN THE 1940s films were so exciting when stars such as Erroll Flynn or Clark Gable filled the screen. They were so gorgeous that women in the audience shrieked with delight.

All the women were very glamorous, with lip-glossed mouths and rippling hair.

Love scenes were tender and romantic, the camera never ventured beyond the bedroom door.

We enjoyed the B-films too. I particularly liked the Edgar Lustgarten semi-documentary crime cases.

There were many inducements to return to the cinema the following week. For one thing Superman was a serial and the trailers poured out exciting blurbs such as:

'You'll thrill to the voice of Deanna Durbin.' 'You'll cry with the victims.' 'You'll laugh with the clowns.' 'You will hate yourself forever if you miss this film.'

When we left the cinema, I would walk backwards to read all the credits on the screen, which were a lot shorter and simpler than they are today.

My mother would urge me to hurry and I would say: "Just a minute mum, I must see who played the part of . . . !"

Outside the cinema there would be queues waiting to go in. Some of them would be looking at the stills from the film displayed in glass cases on the cinema wall.

Maureen Morris

WHEN HOLLYWOOD INVADED OUR VILLAGE

MY FIRST recollection of the flicks was just a wooden hut in the West Yorkshire village where I was brought up.

The air was always blue from the smoke of Woodbines, along with curling pipe smoke. I saw this blue haze rising from the light of the projector and used to think it was part of the cinema projection.

As Hollywood invaded our village we watched those film stars, entranced by their beauty and style - Marlene Dietrich, Greta Garbo, Joan Bennett, Merle Oberon and Jean Arthur. And we mustn't forget red-haired Clara Bow and child star Shirley Temple.

They seemed to be everywhere, as they adorned many souvenirs such as biscuit tins and tea caddies.

I also remember film star biscuits which were chocolate wafers with a card photo of the stars. We swapped these at school so we could get a full set. These cards showed not only the beauties but handsome men such as Wallace Beery and Edward G Robinson. My heroes were Cary Grant and Gregory Peck.

Ladies' hairstyles on the screen were so neat and tidy. To copy the beautifully waved effect my friend and I used to sleep with wave grips all round our heads. We had to fold the pillows under our necks, or the clips would have dug into our head. It was almost impossible to sleep.

Hilda Corner

THE HIGHWAYMAN HAT

I WAS ABSOLUTELY entranced watching Margaret Lockwood in the film The Wicked Lady. I loved her attractive and glamorous highwayman costume with its charming wide-brimmed hat.

Not long after the film was shown, the 'Highwayman Hat' appeared in various hat and clothes shops. Off I went to Marshall and Snelgrove to buy one.

On the following Sunday I proudly wore it to an important church service, and on lots of following occasions. Although the fashion in hats changed as

time went by, I did not get rid of my Highwayman Hat.

During the following years, I wore it, sporting ostrich feathers, with an authentic highwayman costume that I designed and made myself. I won prizes at various carnivals and fancy dress events.

ABOVE: LAURA IN FULL HIGH-WAYMAN GEAR

LEFT: WEARING 'THE HAT'

So today, safely residing in its hatbox, is that copy of the hat which Margaret Lockwood wore in The Wicked Lady 50 years ago!

Laura Fost

BEING JUDY GARLAND

I REMEMBER ONE particular occasion, when I was 14 years old, my grandma came to visit. She was always very critical so when she found fault with the meal my mother cooked, we left her to it and went to the cinema to see Meet Me In St Louis. I was enthralled, so we saw it through twice.

I memorised all the songs and later, when my friends and I were in our garden, I lined up the chairs as in a bus and performed The Trolley Song. At that moment in time I was Judy Garland. .

Vicky Kemp

DOING THE 'DISHES'

I WAS FILM star crazy. I emulated Rita Hayworth and wore my long hair like Veronica Lake's peek-a-boo style.

As my brothers and I did the washing up after Sunday lunch, they would shoot questions at me about current films and their stars. I recited the replies like a devotee.

Later my tastes widened to such charmers as Danny Kaye and Fred Astaire; I was infatuated with several Hollywood actors.

Olwen Evans

THE OLD ONES FROM THE PAST

The old films from the past were best;
Stars that really shone -
Bergman, Garbo, Myrna Loy -
Now all of them have gone.

Who could forget Bette Davis,
That famous movie Queen,
Puffing at a cigarette.
A classic on the screen.

Musical, pure joy to watch
In a world of make believe,
With Fred Astaire and Ginger,
Such magic steps they'd weave.

Gene Kelly dancing in the rain,
A must for all to see,
Captivating young and old
With his faultless artistry.

Cowboy films were favourites,
With the sound of horses' hooves,
Chasing all the bad guys
Who kept falling off the roofs.

They rounded up a posse
To stake out Joe's saloon,
With six guns at the ready
For a shoot-out at high noon.

Oh, yes, they were the best of times,
Our evenings at the flicks,
Munching on our popcorn
In the stalls at one and six.

Margaret Malenoir

PHOTOS OF MY FAVOURITES

IN THE 1940s, when I was a child, I collected cuttings and plastered my bedroom wall with film star photographs. I also used to write to the studios for signed photos of my favourites.

The local chemist shop used to give me their old advertisements which featured stars. Margaret Lockwood and Patricia Roc would frequently be on the ones for Drene shampoo, Max Factor Pan Stik was endorsed by Elizabeth Taylor and several MGM stars. Many stars said they used Lux Toilet Soap.

Margaret Tillett

IN LOVE WITH GLORIA

I GREW UP in Cambridge during the war. I was about 13 when I had my first 'crush' - and it was awful.

I went to the Victoria one evening and saw Two Girls and a Sailor. The story of two show-biz sisters both falling for the same man, it starred Gloria de Haven, June Allyson and Van Johnson, together with a whole host of musical talent which included the Harry James and Xavier Cugat orchestras.

The next day I returned to the Victoria at 1.30pm and had another one-and-ninepence worth; it was a continuous performance and I sat through the whole lot four times.

Emerging at 10.30pm, I was starving and bleary eyed - but I knew every word of the script and every note of the music.

I was also desperately in love with Gloria de Haven. I even wrote to her in Hollywood asking for a pin-up picture, but nothing happened - I guess they were reserved for GIs.

I recovered from Gloria after a few months, but I never recovered from the big band version of Charmaine; it includes what I reckon are the finest 32 bars that Harry James ever played. It still makes the hairs on the back of my neck stand up.

John G Shipcott

☆ *James Mason* ☆

(1909 - 1984)

IN THE 1940s JAMES MASON WAS
EVERYONE'S FAVOURITE SCREEN VILLAIN
IN COSTUME DRAMAS LIKE 'FANNY BY
GASLIGHT' AND 'THE WICKED LADY'.
HIS DISTINCTIVE VOICE AND BROODING
GOOD LOOKS ALMOST TYPECAST HIM
PERMANENTLY.
BUT HE WAS A MUCH MORE VERSATILE
ACTOR AS HE SHOWED IN 'ODD MAN
OUT' IN 1947.
IN THE 1950s HE WAS ABLE TO SHOW HIS
METTLE AS ROMMEL IN BOTH 'THE
DESERT FOX' AND 'THE DESERT RATS'
AND AS JUDY GARLAND'S HUSBAND IN
THE 1954 VERSION OF 'A STAR IS BORN'.
HE CONTINUED WORKING THROUGHOUT
HIS LIFE AND PLAYED VERY MOVINGLY IN
HIS LAST FILM, 'THE SHOOTING PARTY',
RELEASED THE YEAR HE DIED.

Romance
in the dark

THE LOVE SCENES ON THE SCREEN WERE NOT THE ONLY ROMANCES GOING ON WHEN THE LIGHTS WENT DOWN...

THE FIRST TIME

THERE WERE many cinemas open in Preston in October 1942 when I first met my Ted. The prices were: 6d, 9d, ls, 1s 1d, 1s 6d and 1s 10d.

On our second date we went to the New Victoria. We queued for about half an hour before we got into the cinema and then had to queue behind the seats until the lights went on again. These were beautiful lights set in a lovely pattern in the high ceiling. They changed colours every few minutes.

When we were sitting down, I felt a touch on my head as light as a butterfly and as I turned my head to look up at Ted our lips met in our very first kiss, causing my heart to skip a few beats.

I never forgot that first time for the fates decreed we were to be together. As we have now been married for over 50 years, I think they were right.

Eve Clucas

SWEET MEMORIES

ON OUR first date my escort produced a bag of chocolates, not my favourite, but nevertheless a very great treat as sweets were virtually unobtainable during the war.

He never handed me the bag to hold and took it with him at the end of the evening.

Later, after we were married, I asked him why. He then confessed that he had gone into a local sweet shop and told the proprietor that he was taking a girl out for the first time and wanted to make an impression; could she help?

She produced this bag of chocolate gingers, but warned him to wait until we were in the darkness of the cinema before offering me one. They had been standing in the window and had turned a patchy white.

Mary Fieldhouse

HORROR EVERYWHERE

MY MOST memorable and terrifying visit to the cinema was in
London in 1941.

I lived in London and was friendly
with a soldier who was stationed in the
Orkneys. He came home on a short
leave and asked me to go to the pictures
with him. We went to a cinema in the
Edgware Road.

As we left home the air raid sirens
went off and by the time we had gone
on the bus and arrived at the cinema
there was a very noisy raid on. Guns,
bombs and flak were surrounding us -
but in we went.

I had always avoided horror films
and, to my utter dismay, the film showing was a real 'horror'.

Inside we could hear the bombs dropping quite close with their unmistakable
thuds. What with the raid so close and
the awful film, I have never been so terrified in my life.

I don't remember anything about what
the film looked like as I had my eyes
shut tight most of the time, but the talking and sound effects I couldn't shut out.

I was so terrified I was never more
pleased to see the end of the show.
Even going outside with the raid still on,
I felt safer!

Needless to say, I didn't marry this particular soldier and I never told him how
terrified I had been.

Joan Clifford

SOS!

IN LATE May 1944 I was one of very
many squaddies in 'sealed' camps in
southern England awaiting D-Day.

Quite unexpectedly we were
'unsealed' and granted a very short
pass. This enabled me to make a quick
visit home to Hackney, East London.

On arriving at my girlfriend's home I
was told by her mother that she'd gone
to the pictures.

So, still in uniform, I hastened to the
Regal cinema, planning to get a SOS
slide shown on the screen. I had often
seen such slides super-imposed on the
screen and thought it was only a matter
of asking - not so.

The manager was easily found, looking very official in his evening dress and
red carnation, very much in charge of
the queues waiting to get in.

He told me it had to be a very important matter to have a slide shown on the
screen, and made me feel quite mad.

I told him I would try to get a sympa-
thetic ear at the police section house
next door. Almost immediately I found
a more generous side to his nature as he
quickly instructed the slide to be
shown.

My girlfriend came out to the box-
office where I was waiting - and never
did complain about not seeing the end
of the feature film.

We married the following year and we
still cherish together that interrupted
visit to the cinema.

E L Lancaster

WE HAD been going together for about six months when my boyfriend and I decided to get engaged.

On the day in question my boyfriend met me from work. We had just a short time to choose the ring before the jewellers closed.

We then had a cup of tea in town, followed by a visit to the local cinema.

As it was customary in those days to ask a young lady's father if he had any objection to the engagement - the ring in its box was still in my boyfriend's pocket.

After persistently asking him if I could wear it while we were in the cinema, and promising to hand it back when we left, he eventually agreed.

The ring was back in its box when we left the cinema, feeling a little nervous of the task ahead. We needn't have worried, because all went well. Father gave his consent and the ring was, once more, put on my finger, this time to remain.

I'm afraid I never saw the film at all on that occasion. I only had eyes for my lovely new engagement ring.

Winifred Drew

HOLLYWOOD HATS

IN 1935 I was working as a milliner in East London. 'Hollywood hats' - copies of those worn by the famous film stars - were all the rage that year. I made my own Garbo hat in brown fur felt. For my birthday my tailor father had made me a beige suit. I bought a brown jumper to go with it.

Wearing this outfit, I took some cleaning into a recently-opened shop opposite, during my lunch hour.

The good-looking young owner looked me over admiringly.

"Ah, a breath of spring!" he said, adding with a cheeky grin, "And I do like your hat - you ought to have your photograph taken in that!".

I walked out in a daze and went straight into a nearby photographer's studio and had this picture taken.

That was the beginning of our romance and a married life and business partnership which was to last more than 50 happy years.

And, yes, our first shop was a hat shop!

GERTRUDE IN HER 'HOLLYWOOD HAT'

Gertrude Deneberg

COURTING DAYS

THE CINEMA played an important part in our courting days in the 1930s.

It was our highlight of the week, but oh, those interminable queues! I can remember one freezing cold night when there was a buzz of excitement and out came the very resplendently attired commissionaire calling out, "Two for the two and sixes".

We rushed forward, then remembered we couldn't afford it, so fell back in line to stand and freeze a while longer.

We didn't complain, that was life and you accepted it.

Doreen Mayers

A WET AFFAIR

RONALD COLMAN was my pin-up ever since I'd cried my eyes out after seeing him go to the guillotine for love in A Tale of Two Cities.

A couple of years later I had a boyfriend. In fact I had several, but he was the only one with a car. It was a Flying Standard AFU 569, and belonged to his mother. The other boyfriends had bikes!

On Saturday afternoons when half-day school had finished, he'd drive up in this maroon motor and ask my parents' permission to take me to the flicks.

The Ritz at Lincoln was our favourite and for 5s for two, including the price of the tickets, we could have tea in the restaurant before the big picture started.

Fish and chips were ordered. I sat, beaming, in my one and only decent dress, school uniform abandoned for the weekend.

The fish and chips arrived, lovely. I salted and peppered and reached for the vinegar. Being a gentleman, my date decided to do the honours himself. He shook the bottle over my plate, thinking it was a 'shaker'. It wasn't.

The top came off, my plate was drowned in vinegar and so was the rest of me. I was soaked. The puddle under my chair was most embarrassing. I could have killed him.

Am I the only one who sat through four hours of Gone With The Wind with wet pants?

I must have forgiven him. Not long ago we celebrated our 56th wedding anniversary.

Hazel Gill

UNFORGETTABLE

GOING TO the cinema was the best part of my teenage years. You felt so grand, walking on that rich carpet. And in those days you dressed up in silk stockings with seams and high-heeled shoes. It was great, we felt like the stars.

I loved sitting in the back row upstairs - even if it did cost 2s 3d, half my weekly pocket money. If possible I used to go with a boy so I didn't have to pay.

Later I met my husband to be, who was chief operator at the cinema, so I could go in for free. It was 1942 and I remember seeing Yankee Doodle Dandy with James Cagney (one of my favourites) all alone in the cinema as my fiance was running the film through before it was shown.

I always remember that when this film is shown on TV.

Elsie Wilkes

A LOT FOR HALF A CROWN

I WENT TO the pictures every week during the 1930s. It was usually on Monday evenings, that being my half day. I took off on my bicycle, with 2s 6d in my pocket, to my girlfriend's home - 18 miles away.

The two shillings bought two cinema tickets and the remaining sixpence was just enough for a box of chocolates.

The programme usually lasted two and a half to three hours and during that time we were entertained first with the Wurlitzer, followed by the B film and then the 'epic production'.

Some cinemas ran a weekly serial. This called for a major decision, whether to go and see the following instalment the next week - and not such a good main film - or forget the serial and go to the other cinema down the road where a blockbuster was showing.

My parents used to grumble at me for wasting my money on the pictures. But I don't think it was a waste because today, 60 years later, my girlfriend, who has been my wife for over 50 years, still shares her chocolates with me.

F Drinkwater

GOING FOR FREE

I HAD INVITED a young girl to the cinema one night. Somehow I didn't think she would enjoy the Alex which got rather noisy on a Saturday night, so I chose to take her to a better-class cinema in town, the Regal.

The film was The Red Shoes starring Moira Shearer. Much to my horror it turned out to be a romantic weepy about a ballet dancer - not my scene at all - but I did watch it!

She held my hand throughout the show - care, or caution I wonder.

We both enjoyed the evening - and she still remembers it.

Syd Green

THE WAY YOU LOOK TONIGHT

I WAS BARELY 16 when I met Jack, who was a year older. We struck up a warm friendship which developed into a sweet and innocent romance.

One night we went to The Windsor, in Neath, South Wales, to see Ginger Rogers and Fred Astaire - the favourites of the day - in a film called Swingtime. It cost all of 9d to sit in the middle stalls.

Fred sang Just the Way You Look Tonight to Ginger and later Jack wrote all the words out in a letter to me.

A few months later I went away to work in London. We wrote to each other regularly until I had to tell him that I had started to go out with someone else. Someone I've been married to for over 50 years. But I still think tenderly of Jack whenever I hear that song.

Patricia Fox

A PICTURE OF ARTHUR

DURING the war my husband was a Desert Rat serving with General Montgomery. We were married in October 1940 and I didn't see him again until May 1945. Myself and other wives would go months without any mail and not know where our husbands were.

One evening a group of us wives went to the flicks. As we settled into our seats the newsreel was being shown. Suddenly, there on the screen, was my husband crouched by a large gun somewhere in the Western Desert.

I stood up in my seat and shouted, "There's my Arthur!" my heart beating fast and my legs like jelly.

The outcome was that the projectionist took me up to his room, re-ran the newsreel and when I saw my Arthur he cut that part of the film out for me. I had it made into a treasured picture.

Barbara Heyes

Your favourite pin-ups

✪ Ingrid Bergman ✪

(1915 - 1982)

"WHEN THE CAMERA MOVES IN ON THE
BERGMAN FACE, AND SHE'S SAYING
SHE LOVES YOU, IT WOULD MAKE
ANYBODY LOOK ROMANTIC." SO SAID
HUMPHREY BOGART ON FILMING WITH
HER IN 'CASABLANCA'.
THE SWEDISH-BORN ACTRESS WAS NOT
THE FIRST CHOICE FOR THE FILM, NOR
WAS BOGART. THE LEADS SHOULD HAVE
BEEN PLAYED BY ANN SHERIDAN AND
RONALD REAGAN!
A STRING OF SUCCESSFUL FILMS FOL-
LOWED BUT IN 1950 SCANDAL STRUCK.
SHE WAS MARRIED TO A SWEDISH DOCTOR
BUT GAVE BIRTH TO DIRECTOR ROBERTO
ROSSELLINI'S CHILD.
OSTRACISED IN HOLLYWOOD, SHE MADE
FILMS IN ITALY AND FRANCE UNTIL SHE
WON AN OSCAR FOR HER 'COMEBACK' FILM
'ANASTASIA' IN 1956.

Film buffs

INTO A WORLD OF MAKE-BELIEVE

MY FAVOURITE form of escape was the cinema. From 1939 to 1960 my life, like that of most of my generation, was centred round nightly visits to the cinema.

My grandma took me to see my first film in 1939 at the Rialto in Sheepridge. I was five. She had been told by my father that there was a wonderful film being shown about a monkey. Thinking it was a Walt Disney film similar to Bambi and Pinocchio, she said she would take me.

When we arrived we sat in the best seats at the back of the cinema. She never went to the front, that was for the common people!

The film being shown was King Kong and from the moment 'he' appeared on screen she was a frightened, trembling heap. I loved it!

She managed to watch until King Kong appeared on the Empire State Building banging his chest - and that was it. She let out one scream, grabbed me and ran up the aisle. She demanded to see the manager and told him his film was disgusting and so was he. My grandma was only about 4 feet 11

MAUREEN AT 16 IN 1952 WHEN SHE IMAGINED HERSELF AS ALL THE STARS ROLLED INTO ONE!

inches and weighed six stone, but she whacked him with a rolled-up umbrella and said she would never darken the door of his cinema again.

I cried all the way home because she hadn't let me see the end of it.

My father thought it was all hilarious.

Every Saturday afternoon we would visit the Regent and queue up with lots of other children to watch a couple of hours of films.

All the boys wore little gun belts with toy silver guns, and when the Indians or baddies appeared, they pulled out the guns and shouted "Bang, bang!" as they leapt up and down in their seats.

In the early 1950s girls all contrived to have big busts, small waists and curvy hips. Jane Russell, Marilyn Monroe, Anita Eckberg, Gina Lollobrigida and Mamie Van Doren were the pin-ups we all had to emulate.

To achieve this we had circle-stitched bras which a normal bosom wouldn't fit into, so we would put cotton wool in. When we put on our tight sweaters our boobs stood out like chapel hat pegs.

If we didn't use cotton wool, we could be left with a concave bosom if the centres of the bra were pushed in because someone had pushed past you, or you'd bumped into something.

We also wore girdles to make our tummies flatter and our waists thinner. They were boned, so sitting down wasn't easy, but the finished result looked fashionable and in keeping with the fifties.

Hairstyles then were dictated by the stars. At different times during that decade I had a bubble cut, a la Lollobrigida, with curls all over my head.

The gamine look made popular by Audrey Hepburn influenced many of the Huddersfield girls, because at the time she was engaged to Jimmy Hanson, the son of the Huddersfield tycoon.

We had a wonderful hairdresser called Vera Moore who had a salon down Imperial Arcade, Huddersfield. She had a window full of portraits of the stars and when they visited Hudderfield's Theatre Royal, they would have their hair coiffured by her.

The big Gainsborough stars of the 1940s - Margaret Lockwood, Phyllis Calvert, Jean Kent, Patricia Roc, Anne Crawford - all had their portraits on display, signed 'To Vera Moore with many thanks'.

They were left there for many years for people to ogle at.

Maureen Dyson

IN LOVE WITH THE ELEPHANT BOY

WHILE LIVING in London with my grandparents, mother and sister in the 1930s, we were taken as a treat on Saturdays to Wembley for tea at Lyons Corner House, then to the pictures. So began my life-long love of the cinema.

We saw musicals with Alice Faye and Sonja Henie, but the film of this time that made the most impression was The Elephant Boy with Sabu. He became my first celluloid love, soon to be replaced by Gene Autry the singing cowboy and his horse Champion.

When my mother married again we moved to Greenford where my sister and I used to go to the Saturday morning children's cinema. My grandmother came with us once but all the shouting proved too much for her and she said 'never again'.

During our three-year evacuation to the Midlands, visits to the cinema became a thing of the past. It was not until we returned to live with our grandparents at Clacton in 1943 that we could take up picture-going once again.

In 1944 I left school and started my first job in a shop. At this time there were three cinemas in Clacton ranging from the high class Century, the slightly lower Odeon, down to the Essoldo which was known locally as the fleapit.

Although terrible things were happening in the world at war, it was actually a wonderful time to be young and pretty.

Clacton was full of the armed forces of many nations and it was not often I paid for my own cinema seat, though it was always the film I was interested in!

And what films I saw, far too many to list here. And the stars: lovely leading ladies such as Hedy Lamarr, Greer Garson, Irene Dunne, Betty Grable and Maria Moutez fluttering long eye lashes at Alan Ladd, Gary Cooper, Cary Grant, Tyrone Power and many more.

I wrote to many of the stars and had a large collection of signed photographs.

When I married in 1949 I returned to the Midlands. As a break from my growing family I would leave my husband to babysit and go by bus to the cinema. Later on I took the children to see such films as Mary Poppins and The Sound of Music then they, too, became film fans.

Audrey M Davis

A MAGICAL MYSTERY TOUR

I N THE years before the Second World War, money was tight and we deemed ourselves lucky if my mother could scrape a few pence together to allow us to go to the cinema.

Afternoon matinees cost one or two pennies, depending on where you sat. It was a blessed relief to many parents to get a break from their offspring.

For the children it was a wild and exciting transportation into the world of films, whether it be a western or musical.

When I left school at 14 and went to work, my small allowance of pocket money was mainly spent on films I wanted to see.

Most weekends I went with my workmates to the larger cinemas in Birmingham. The films, particularly the musicals, were real morale boosters during the dark days of the war - the glamour of the stars, spectacular costumes, wonderful choreography and the sheer joy of natural talent.

Coming home from work during the week, my obsession with the cinema had me jumping off the train as soon as it pulled into the station and racing to the local cinema - many times missing a meal to do so. Films I particularly liked I

would see two or three times and I felt sad when they ended.

For many thousands of my generation the films were a magical mystery tour. We were hooked on the real talent shown in musicals of the time - dancers such as Donald O'Connor, Peggy Ryan, Gene Kelly, Fred Astaire, Cyd Charisse, and Ann Miller were unsurpassed.

Then there were the beautiful voices of Ann Blyth, Deanna Durbin, Kathryn Grayson, Vivian Blaine, Ginny Simms and countless more.

There were also horror films to haunt you into sleepless nights - then soon forgotten.

Now I view the old films in the comfort of my own home on television, reliving the memories of my youth with the same enthusiasm.

Olive Adams

WHERE DREAMS CAME TRUE

M Y FIRST experience of the silver screen was at the Saturday morning Mickey Mouse Club when I was about eight. I was captivated right from the start by this wonderful world of the movies where dreams came true and the mundane world was forgotten.

Imagine a hundred or so eight to ten-year-olds at the pictures. It was pandemonium until the lights went down, then all eyes were on the screen and you could hear a pin drop as we were all enthralled and lost in a world of wonder.

The cinema manager used to lead us from the stage in our Mickey Mouse ditty:

"Every Saturday morning where do we go?
Getting into mischief, oh, dear no!
To the Mickey Mouse Club
With our badges on,

Just around the corner at the Odeon."

When I was about twelve I graduated to the 'big pictures'. The trouble was, money was hard to come by. My main source of income was the collection of rabbit skins and jam jars from relatives. These were hurriedly rushed to the local rag and bone man, praying he would come across with enough coppers for my entrance fee.

If the main feature was 'A' certificate I would stand outside asking each adult if they would take me in. Someone always did, but we would part company once inside.

After the news, cartoon and B movie we came to the main feature. It was very much the star system in those days and we all had our favourites whose films would never miss.

Oh, yes, I had my idols: Bing Crosby with his easy manner and wonderful voice; Clark Gable, the handsome one in San Francisco and Gone With the Wind; Ronald Colman, what charm he had in The Prisoner of Zenda and A Tale of Two Cities and Humphrey Bogart the tough guy in The Maltese Falcon and Casablanca - but how many remember him in Dead End?

Of course, as I got older, the lady stars came into the reckoning and I fell in love with them all: Ginger Rogers, Dorothy Lamour, Doris Day and, the queen of them all, Ingrid Bergman.

The first signs that I was showing interest in the opposite sex was when I removed the picture of my boxing hero Tommy Farr from my bedroom wall and replaced him with a gorgeous picture of Ingrid Berman.

I am retired now and, what luck, I live a few hundred yards from our local cinema, the oldest in Suffolk, at Leiston. I still go every week.

Colin White

A CINEMA IN THE DESERT

M Y MOTHER went to the pictures when film-going was in its infancy. The first shows in Liverpool were held in the Picton Hall and my parents, who were courting at the time, took my maternal grandmother with them one night.

The film was one of the villain chucking the poor girl and her baby out into the snow variety. Grandmother got so angry at this treatment that she leapt to her feet and shouted, "You leave her alone" - to my parents confusion no doubt!

My first visits were to the Saturday matinees. Punctuated by shouts of "Look behind you!" it would seem that the quality of films hadn't advanced a great deal.

Later on, after a visit to Blackpool, I became something of an organ addict and chose the cinema because it had an organ, rather than the film.

When war broke out I was a policeman and my cinema visits became regulated by the Luftwaffe. My intended wife was a nurse and on the infrequent days we got together we went to the Liverpool Paramount, now the Odeon. If you got there before 4pm the flat charge was 1s 6d.

If there was an air-raid warning in operation when the show finished, the organist would reappear and play for dancing in the aisles.

After the May blitz in 1941, which brought the city transport to a standstill, we were wondering how we were going to get to the city centre cinema. We noticed a slightly-damaged fire engine standing on the opposite side of the road. It turned out that a friend was driving it so we went down into town clinging to the back rail.

Our arrival at the Paramount bought a panicking doorman rushing out. He seemed bemused when we stepped down and asked if there were any seats available.

Later on I joined the Commandos and duly arrived in Gibraltar. Here I'm sure I lost of couple of pounds in an overheated cinema watching Wuthering Heights.

Over in Algeria I experienced another kind of cinema. The dialogue was in French, the top quarter of the screen was obliterated by English subtitles and the bottom quarter by Arabic ones.

During the show the air was rent with the female attendants running up and down shouting "Defens de fumer!" as the lads tried to light fags under their gas capes.

When the war in Africa finished we moved to Alexandria. One night we were driven to a cinema in the desert. It was open air, the walls were old wooden railway sleepers, so was the seating and the film broke down so many times that I'm sure no one knew what it had been about at the end.

Down by the Red Sea I watched Desert Victory seated on a petrol tin and wrapped in a blanket against the cold. The screen was unrolled on the side of a mobile cinema.

Then the invasion of France took place. I was one of 20 prisoners of war marched by the Germans to a cinema. We wondered why the Germans were being so kind to us - then we realised that it was an attempt to discourage us; the newsreel was all about the invasion.

The film showed happy, laughing Wehrmacht troops driving passed shot-up Allied tanks, which was all very well but they looked very like the same tanks taken from various angles.

The whole effect was ruined when the camera panned the horizon - you couldn't see it for the massed shipping. We came away from that performance feeling very happy.

A few years ago I saw the film Out of Africa in a Luxembourg cinema. I sat in the most luxurious armchair - style seat, like nothing I have ever seen. I almost made them an offer for it - the seat, not the cinema!

Tom Jones

THUMBING THROUGH THE MOVIE MAGAZINES

I FIRST WENT to the cinema in 1935 with my parents to see their favourite comedian Will Hay in Boys Will Be Boys.

I soon became hooked and started going to the flicks regularly with school friends.

A highlight of the week was dashing round to our local newsagent on publication day of the movie magazines, Picture Show and Picturegoer, and thumbing through the pages to find out the release dates of the latest films.

I also waited eagerly for my father to open his Players cigarette packets so that I could add illustrated pictures of famous film stars to my collection.

During school holidays I helped the projectionist at one of our cinemas to change the showcases on a Sunday morning. I also watched, from the projection box, films run through the projector from the giant reel.

Saturday mornings were always kept free for the Odeon Boys and Girls Club - the president being the 'guv'nor' himself, J Arthur Rank. He lived near Winchester and considered the Odeon we went to as his local cinema.

Films I particularly enjoyed were Gone With the Wind, The Adventures of Robin Hood, Casablanca, Great Expectations and Genevieve.

Film music also played an important part in my earlier filmgoing days and the stirring musical score by Erich Wolfgang Korngold for The Adventures of Robin Hood has always remained vivid in my mind.

A resident organist played most evenings at the Odeon. Slides would flash on the screen so that the audience could join in the chorus of popular songs. One organist was sacked for playing A Lovely Bunch of Coconuts on a Sunday evening!

I'm still crazy about films and even today I distribute brochures for the Screen Cinema in Winchester. The Theatre Royal is closed for refurbishment but all being well, I shall be back there again arranging displays for the new showcases.

Phil Yates

THE VIOLIN FOR LOVE

I STARTED GOING to the flicks at the tender age of seven in 1925. I was taken along by my mother, who was an enthusiastic filmgoer, on Saturdays nights for the simple reason that she didn't want to leave me alone at home.

In those early years there were no lower age limits for viewing films and no classification, although the Hays Office set the standards.

I found it an extraordinary experience since the silent cinema in those days was truly a dream factory where the audience took part vocally in the screen action by laughter, booing, cheering, mock sighing and crying - particularly the ladies who seemed to respond more easily to the tender scenes.

Music was provided by a small orchestra of three players who synchronised the instruments and pieces to the mood being shown on the screen above them. It was usually the violin for love scenes, the drum for drama and for pistol shots and the piano for general scenes, including rapid movements.

I remember Charlie Chaplin in The Gold Rush where he caused howls of laughter by being so hungry in a cabin that constantly teetered on the edge of a precipice, but eating, with great delicacy, part of one of his over-sized boots.

We thrilled to Rudolf Valentino sweeping through the desert on his Arab steed to make love to a beautiful female in a huge tent (great sighs from the ladies in the audience) and later to carry her off (rather uncomfortably, I thought) to his desert palace.

Cowboys were very much in action with characters such as William S Hart, Tom Mix with his wonderful horse and the vigorous Buck Jones - all of whom were excellent gunslingers.

The event of the talkies changed the style and audience participation virtually died out. My first talkie was Al Jolson in The Jazz Singer - a young woman on my left wept profusely as he sang Sonny Boy.

Lawrence Marson

GLAMOUR AND FANTASY

FOR ME the heyday of the cinema was in the 1940s and 50s when I was growing up. I became an ardent film fan after seeing my first Shirley Temple picture, progressing later to the lavish musicals and all the other memorable Hollywood films that featured the famous stars.

Perhaps my two most poignant recollections of those times are of the Pathe News and the magnificent cinema organs that were played during the intervals. Both were essential parts of the double-feature programmes.

Remember that crowing cock heralding the start of the news, followed by the distinctive male voice, always the same one, describing the wartime triumphs and disasters? Or, in peacetime, the more mundane scenes of the boat race or royalty at Ascot?

The news feature was very important for us then as it portrayed what otherwise we could only read about in newspapers or listen to on the wireless.

Then, of course, the national anthem was always played at the end of the final performance and I can remember how the plush swing-seats snapped back almost in unison as everybody stood up.

The exceptions were those of the couples in the back rows who, taken by surprise, had to struggle to disentangle themselves and put their seats back quietly.

I wish I'd kept my piles of film magazines and my prized album with all the photographs of my idols, for they would have been collectors' items now but, more than that, they would be mementos of the many happy hours I spent in the magical atmosphere of the old picture palaces.

Pat Box

A CHILLING MOMENT

IT WAS war time. I was eight years old and living with my aunt and uncle in Collyweston, a small village in Northamptonshire. Village life was usually uneventful so that I had been looking forward to this day for several weeks. Not only were we to go over to King's Cliffe for dinner with Aunt Violet and tea with Aunt Rose but there was also to be a film show for children at the Scout hut.

I set off early on foot. Aunt Lil would follow later on her bike and give me a lift on the back for the last few miles. I had almost reached the soldiers' check point at the cross roads before the bike caught me up, which was just as well as Aunt Lil had my identity card.

"Will you be coming to the film show, Auntie?" I asked, as we started off down the road with me sitting well back on the bike's saddle, while Aunt Lil made do with the narrow bit at the front.

"No. It's for children. Roger and the others will go with you, and me and Aunt Violet will be able to put our feet up for a bit."

We arrived at Aunt Violet's in time to see the joint arriving, hot and juicy from the baker's down the road while crisp roast potatoes and a golden Yorkshire pudding, its sides curled high, were brought out from the oven of the range in the kitchen.

After dinner, with coins pressed into our hands, the cousins and I made our way down the lane to the Scout hut. There was a good turnout and an excited audience packed into the small room. When it was time, the light was switched off and there were little squeals as the small screen in front of our rows of wooden chairs flickered into life.

Black and white images appeared before us with a caption at the bottom of the screen to tell us what was happening and what people were saying. The picture was sometimes jerky and its surface danced with scratchy lights, but we all sat engrossed in the story.

The film concerned a magician who performed his magic tricks on stage. The climax of his act came when a volunteer from his audience was put into an upright decorated box and knives were plunged up to their hilts through slits in the sides. The knives were then withdrawn, the box opened, and the smiling victim revealed to be completely unhurt.

How we all clapped and cheered. The magician was persuaded to do an encore and, as he helped another volunteer into the box and inserted the knives, we sat in happy anticipation waiting to clap and cheer even louder. But this time when the knives were withdrawn they were running with blood and an uneasy silence settled over the audience in the little hut.

When the box was opened and the man inside was shown to be dead, I felt Roger's hand creep into mine and I held it tightly. To a child whose only experience of the cinema to date had been, The Bluebird of Happiness and Dumbo The Flying Elephant, this was a chilling moment.

I don't know how the others fared for, by some silent pact, we never spoke about it afterwards, not even to the grown-ups, but I had some very bad dreams in the weeks that followed and could not be persuaded anywhere near a cinema for several years.

Margaret Thomas

ORANGES AND FISH AND CHIPS

DURING THE Great War I was at school. Mother started taking me and my brother to the pictures every week. We went to an old music hall in Oldbury which had been turned into a picture house. I think it cost 6d for mother and 3d each for me and my brother. We sat on very hard benches among the smell of oranges and fish and chips.

When the projector occasionally broke down there were shouts and boos from the audience until the picture came on again.

When I started courting the talkies were well advanced. The first film my future wife and I saw together was King Kong with a supporting film called So This Is Harris with Phil Harris and his band. Because Harris was also my name, this supporting film gave us a laugh for many years to come.

Our uncle worked for Pat Collins the fairground showman, and uncle told us that he was one of the first men to show moving pictures, which he did on the fairground.

Alfred Harris

SWAPSY WITH OUR FOOD

GOING TO the cinema was pure escapism, a chance to lose yourself in a world that could never be yours. My first recollection was going with my family at the age of five, though I'm told I'd often been before in my mother's arms.

Us kids would trot off any time we could. We welcomed my mother having to work as this meant we had to be occupied so we wouldn't get into trouble.

The flicks opened at 1 o'clock and shut about 10 o'clock. It was a continuous performance so we could watch the same films over and over again.

In the early days of my cinema visits the lights never went up, so in the boring bits, probably the news, we would take the opportunity to stretch our legs and walk up to the back and spy on the courting couples sitting in the back row.

It was quite an event to get ready to go to the flicks. You had to take your tuck, which was usually carried in a paper carrier bag and consisted of a bottle of drink made from lemonade powder and water, a Nestle milk sandwich, 1d bag of Smiths broken crisps and a lump of mum's bread pudding.

Sometimes we did swapsy with our food during the performance, only to receive a clout round the ear from someone behind for making a noise.

I loved the musicals and have fond memories of my favourites like Ann Miller, Sue Ellen, Betty Grable and, of course, Gene Kelly - the best of them all. Then there was Ann Blyth with her beautiful skin and lovely smile.

I vividly remember seeing the life story of Jeanette Scott, the daughter of Thora Hird, showing her beautiful frilly bedroom, pretty clothes and tons of lovely shoes in all styles and colours.

How jealous I was of her not having to share a bed with her two sisters (as I did) and not having to wear cardboard in her shoes until her dad could afford the leather to mend them.

On a Friday mum always had extra money and we could have an ice-cream when the usherette came round with her tray. She walked up and down the aisle in the dark with just a torch to see her way.

The ice-creams were delicious in small waxed tubs and we used to bend the lid in half and use it as a spoon. And then there was delicious Kia-ora orange drink, or Orange Maid iced lollies, or thick dark chocolate around a block of Lyons Maid ice cream - wonderful!

I loved the cinema - the opulence, grandeur and sheer escapism from the very ordinary, poor life we led!

Gillian Price

A FILM AT THE READY

WHILE SERVING in the British Army in India in the 1920s, my father, an avid cinema buff, nearly always managed to get himself involved with cinemas wherever he was posted, usually as a projectionist.

My earliest recollection as a very small child was of a grand cinema hall in Bangalore in Southern India. This was owned by a rich Parsee gentleman who was equally enthusiastic about this modern magical phenomenon.

His picture palace was all Victorian baroque. The best seats, reserved for the 'better class' in the audience, were in stuffed sofas up front, and customers occupying these plush seats were expected to attend in formal evening dress.

The high society sense of the occasion was enhanced when they arrived in a gharry - a horse-drawn carriage driven by an Indian coachman, smartly turned out in a uniform of sorts topped with an impeccable rolled turban.

As very small children my sister and I were not allowed to stay up for these functions but we became fleeting film stars whenever a film was on show.

A photograph of the two of us, dressed in our white night-gowns and holding lighted candles aloft, was flashed on the screen at the end of the film. This bore the caption 'Good night' to indicate that the evening's entertainment was over.

A load of advertising material used to be sent to my father in advance of the films to be shown.

Harold Lloyd was a popular favourite with the audience and once, when one of his comedies was the coming attraction, the town was flooded with cardboard horn-rimmed glasses. A blown-up photograph of the star, dangling from a huge clockface, was displayed in our front window.

Subsequent Army postings for my father never failed to reveal an opportunity for becoming involved in the cinema. His last assignment before retiring from the Army was to a small hill station, situated near Poona, too small to boast of a hall big enough to show films.

Not to be beaten, my father rigged up a hand projector in an open-air ball alley. There we sat, under the stars, watching the cream of the Hollywood movies, enthralled, in dead silence except for the sound of my father laboriously cranking the handle behind us.

Slapstick comedies were favourites with my sister and me - we were too young to wallow in the syrupy romances turned out by the film makers.

Later, though, as a young schoolgirl I became the envy of my peers when I wrote for and obtained a signed photograph of my favourite film star - Laura La Plante.

Olive Monkcom

NEVER A HAIR OUT OF PLACE

I REMEMBER BEING taken to a local cinema called the Lyceum in Garston in the early 1940s. Garston was a bus ride away from where we lived at Speke (Liverpool).

The Lyceum had another name, not very complimentary - The Bughouse. Some customers claimed you went in with a cardigan and came out with a jumper, we never did however. My two older brothers, Frank and Stan, were in charge of me.

Quite often during the performance, the projector would develop a fault and the film stopped. You had to sit forward pretty quickly when this happened, because more often than not, the person behind would kick the back of your seat and start yelling "Get the film back on". The noise was deafening.

The heroine never had a hair out of place or her make-up ruined, even after the most strenuous adventures, and all the men fighting and rolling around the floor, never lost their hats. We used to hope they would!

Even the cowboys in the Western films were clean and tidy at the end of a gruelling ride or gunfight.

We loved going to the Lyceum and hated the time when we had to leave our seats at the end of the show.

We had many discussion about the films after our night out, so the magic didn't end with leaving the cinema, it kept us talking for days afterwards.

Doreen Ellison

THE CURTAINS IN FLAMES

I STARTED GOING to the cinema when I was nine, in 1923. On Saturdays we were given 4d to go to the children's matinee at 2pm. We each had a halfpenny to buy a sherbert dab.

I loved the excitement of going to the pictures. The silent films in black and white, with printing that came up on the screen describing the action or dialogue. Sometimes it went up so fast I couldn't read it all, but it didn't spoil my enjoyment.

I remember Pearl White mouthing silent screams as she hung from a cliff, or was tied to railway lines with the steam train puffing nearer and nearer, then at the vital moment it came up on the screen, 'to be continued next week'.

I saw Lillian and Dorothy Gish in Orphans of the Storm in floods of tears. I was in love with Rudolph Valentino and dreamed of being carried away on a camel to a tent in the desert.

I never cared for Charlie Chaplin, but Harold Lloyd in impossible situations I thought very funny.

In my teens I worked in London in domestic service, in Wimbledon. I often went to the cinema on my half day. At that time,1932, Reginald Forte played the great organ that rose up in front of the screen before the performance.

Once I was at the Regal in Wimbledon. Reginald was playing the 1812 overture and he was at the part where the city was in flames. We saw it on the screen, the guns were blasting and the church bells ringing. Suddenly one of the curtains at the side of the screen burst into flames. I never knew if it were an accident or a deliberate effect.

Loretta Young, Myrna Loy, Katharine Hepburn, Norma Shearer, Jessie Matthews, Vivien Leigh and Gracie Fields - how I longed to be as beautiful as them!

I did wear my little hat tipped over one eye like Myrna Loy. I sent for a lovely full-skirted dance dress like one Ginger Rogers wore, but it took me so long to pay for it at 1s a week, I never did it again.

My favourite male stars were Paul Robeson, George Raft, Clark Gable, Jack Buchanan, Ronald Colman and Bing Crosby. I loved romantic films.

In 1936 I got married, babies arrived, and my visits to the cinema were very few and far between, but I did cycle five or six miles to the nearest town to see Gone With The Wind.

What a wonderful film. I have seen it twice on television; I never tire of it.

Gwen Gray

NOTHING QUITE LIKE IT

I GREW UP in Newport in Wales, a town which once boasted ten cinemas.

With over fifty years of cinema-going behind me, I look back with relish at a misspent youth at the flicks.

From being met by my mum, out of junior school, and taken to see Walt Disney's Bambi (and crying when the mother deer was shot), to as recently as being educated and deeply moved by Steven Spielberg's Amistad.

All through those years, films and the cinema have been an integral part of my life.

I have experienced every emotion at the pictures. Laughing, crying (sometimes in the same scene), shock, rapture, horror. And oh! Those wonderful American musicals! The sort where you walked home singing all the songs, and went straight to the music shop the next day to buy the LP!

As a teenager, I was warned by dad to be careful about seeing Rock Around The Clock. He'd heard reports in the paper about jiving in the aisles and sure enough dad was right! When the dancing broke out, my friend and I ran home as fast as our legs could carry us.

That all seems rather tame in today's world, but things were different in the fifties. In those days, if a boy wanted to make a big impression on a girl, he would take her into the 'posh' seats upstairs and buy her a box of chocolates.

This happened to me when I was seventeen. I clung grimly onto the box of Black Magic, because I wanted to give them to my mum. Sadly, I don't remember the names of either the boy or the film!

There was a mystique and glamour about the stars of the past, which was kept alive by the film magazines.

I regularly bought copies of Picturegoer (weekly) and Photoplay (monthly). The Film Review could be bought only from cinemas, that was also a monthly.

For me, cinema has something that no other medium has. It has the power to transport ordinary folks away from their hum-drum lives, into a magic world of make believe.

What can compare to settling into your seat at the pictures. The lights go down. The air of excitement and expectancy builds up. The music washes over you and you are lost in another world. TV and video may be cosy and convenient, but nothing is quite the same as the flicks!

Frances Oakendon

VOTE TO SEE THE STARS

I N MY YOUTH I used to visit the cinema at least twice a week, sometimes three times, in the 1940s and 50s.

Later when I met the young lady who was to become my wife, we had one thing in common - we both loved going to the cinema.

When I was 17, in July 1947, I was given the bookmark shown here at the Adelphi cinema at Bulwell in Nottinghamshire. As you can see it was asking for support for Sunday cinema. Needless to say I voted for it.

R A Marsden

BOOK MARK

JAMES MASON

VOTE
for
SUNDAY CINEMAS
on
FRIDAY, JULY 18th, 1947
———
From 12 noon to 8 p.m.
———
RECORD YOUR VOTE AT
Polling Stations as Advertised

I F YOU want to see your favourite Film Star on Sundays at your local cinema YOU

MUST VOTE

This may be your last chance

Don't Waste It

Go to Your Usual Polling Station and mark your Ballot Paper thus:

ARE YOU FOR OR AGAINST SUNDAY ENTERTAINMENT	FOR	AGAINST
	X	

Tell your friends

DON'T LEAVE IT TO THE OTHER PERSON

YOU ARE THE OTHER PERSON

Issued by the Notts. Sunday Cinema Association

BOTH SIDES OF A BOOKMARK URGING CINEMAGOERS TO VOTE TO SEE UP-TO-DATE FILMS, RATHER THAN OLD ONES, ON A SUNDAY

IN JANUARY 1940, at 14, I started my first job in a factory on war work. For me the cinema became the main escape from the stark reality of work, the Battle of Britain and, later, the Blitz.

For 9d, 1s or 1s 3d you entered the glamorous dream world of film.

The war dampened the excitement of our teenage years and the normal development into adulthood. For me Mickey Rooney in the Andy Hardy series portrayed what the youth of Britain was missing. Here were carefree college teenagers enjoying their cars and innocent love affairs under the firm, but understanding guidance of Judge Hardy, the father played by actor Lewis Stone.

The stream of Andy's girlfriends were played by Judy Garland, Lana Turner, Esther Williams, Kathryn Grayson, Donna Reed, Ann Rutherford and Bonita Granville - all beautiful young girls who were the envy of a young film-goer.

The cinema was the place to take and court a girlfriend. Dressed in your best clothes, it was a special social occasion - but as often as not you had to queue in the foyer to get in.

My wife of 50 years shared our first date watching Bette Davis in Now Voyager.

Later, when I was called up in 1944, my leaves were spent going 'up West' in London to see the latest films. We would sit in the cinema with courting couples who would include American, Polish, Free French, Dutch, Norwegians, Belgium and Commonwealth servicemen.

The doodlebug and V2 rocket replaced the bombs to disturb the sound track.

After demob we continued our courtship with a weekly visit to the cinema, and when we married, an outing to the pictures was a must on our honeymoon.

This love affair with the cinema continued into the television era, until the films became of the 'kitchen sink' type.

Those days of the handsome and glamorous film stars and the Hay's censorship code, remain with us with warm affection and nostalgia.

Chris Tolley

☆ *Clark Gable* ☆

(1901 - 1960)

"FRANKLY, MY DEAR, I DON'T GIVE A
DAMN" - EVERYONE KNOWS WHO SAID
THAT AND IN WHAT FILM. YET CLARK
GABLE DIDN'T WANT THE PART OF
RHETT BUTLER IN 'GONE WITH THE
WIND' BECAUSE HE DIDN'T GET ON
WITH THE DIRECTOR.
HE HADN'T HAD MUCH CHOICE ABOUT HIS
ROLE IN A PREVIOUS FILM EITHER -
'IT HAPPENED ONE NIGHT' WITH
CLAUDETTE COLBERT - HE WAS 'LENT'
BY MGM TO COLUMBIA STUDIOS. BUT
HE WAS LUCKY, BOTH HE AND HIS
CO-STAR WON OSCARS FOR THEIR ROLES.
A FORMER OIL-DRILLER AND LUMBERJACK
WITH EARS THAT WERE TOO BIG - HE
BECAME FILMGOERS' FAVOURITE LEADING
MAN IN THE 1930s AND 40s AND WAS
KNOWN AS THE KING OF HOLLYWOOD.